BUDGET TRAVEL GUIDE

STOCKHOLM
'92-'93 ON $50 A DAY

by Alice Garrard

PRENTICE HALL TRAVEL

NEW YORK • LONDON • TORONTO • SYDNEY • TOKYO • SINGAPORE

FROMMER BOOKS

Published by Prentice Hall General Reference
A division of Simon & Schuster Inc.
15 Columbus Circle
New York, NY 10023

ISBN 0-13-334699-4
ISSN 1055-534X

Design by Robert Bull Design
Maps by Geografix Inc.

Manufactured in the United States of America

FROMMER'S STOCKHOLM ON $50 A DAY
Editor-in-Chief: Marilyn Wood
Senior Editor: Judith de Rubini
Editors: Alice Fellows, Paige Hughes, Theodore Stavrou
Assistant Editors: Suzanne Arkin, Peter Katucki, Lisa Renaud
Managing Editor: Leanne Coupe

CONTENTS

APPENDIX 148

INDEX 153

LIST OF MAPS

INVITATION TO THE READERS

In researching this book, I have come across many wonderful establishments, the best of which I have included here. I am sure that many of you will also come across appealing hotels, inns, restaurants, guest houses, shops, and attractions. Please don't keep them to yourself. Share your experiences, especially if you want to comment on places that have been included in this edition that have changed for the worse. You can address your letters to:

Alice Garrard
Frommer's Stockholm '92–'93 on $50 a Day
c/o Prentice Hall Travel
15 Columbus Circle
New York, NY 10023

A DISCLAIMER

Readers are advised that prices fluctuate in the course of time and travel information changes under the impact of the varied and volatile factors that affect the travel industry. Neither the author nor the publisher can be held responsible for the experiences of readers while traveling. Readers are invited to write to the publisher with ideas, comments, and suggestions for future editions.

SAFETY ADVISORY

Whenever you're traveling in an unfamiliar city or country, stay alert. Be aware of your immediate surroundings. Wear a moneybelt and keep a close eye on your possessions. Be particularly careful with cameras, purses, and wallets, all favorite targets of thieves and pickpockets.

INTRODUCING STOCKHOLM

Stockholm perches near the top of the world, dotted across numerous islands in the Baltic Sea and the crystal-clear waters of Lake Mälaren. On a map she appears cool and aloof in that far-away world. Up close she is a modern ideal.

In no other city do human beings and nature coexist so harmoniously, nor does the Old World meet the New so gracefully. Stockholm is Scandinavia's most beautiful capital city; indeed, she ranks high on the "World's Loveliest Cities" list, this City on the Water, this Jewel of the North. Even the subways here have been turned into art galleries.

The tiny, meandering streets of Gamla Stan (Old Town) complement the vast openness of Skansen, an outdoor museum where the past blooms again. At night, the city kicks up her heels in glamorous clubs that mix music, sophistication, and merriment. Restaurants bow to the world's tastes.

Stockholm's beauty is not just relegated to its natural setting and architecture. The Swedish people are warm and hospitable; their openness and warmth, endless. You'll wish your stay here could be.

---

1. GEOGRAPHY, HISTORY & BACKGROUND

GEOGRAPHY

Visually, Stockholm ranks among the world's most beautiful cities. Liken it to a beautiful woman reclining on a chaise longue of 14

WHAT'S SPECIAL ABOUT STOCKHOLM

Islands
☐ Gamla Stan, where history is alive in centuries-old buildings and streets.
☐ Djurgården, the Deer Park of the kings, a pocket of pure country in the middle of the city.

Awards
☐ Nobel Prizes, awarded annually since 1901.
☐ The Water Prize, inspired by the Nobel Prizes, encourages conservation of water; awarded since 1991.

For the Kids
☐ Skansen, an open-air museum and zoo.
☐ The Marionette Museum, with puppets from around the world, some that say "please touch."

Museums
☐ The Vasa Museum, built around a ship that sank on its maiden voyage in 1628

Square
☐ Kungsträdgården, site of concerts in summer and ice skating in winter, a popular meeting spot year round.

Shopping
☐ Beautiful crystal, Orrefors and Kosta Boda, fills Stockholm's shops.

Buildings
☐ City Hall, with its square tower topped with three crowns.
☐ Globe Arena, the tallest spherical construction in the world.

Festival
☐ Lucia, the festival of light, on December 10.

Beaches
☐ They are not close to downtown, they are *in* downtown.

Hostels
☐ Among them, a three-masted schooner and a former prison.

Nightlife
☐ Jazz and blues thrive in such clubs as Stampen and Mosebacke, and if you come early, it's often free.

Literary Shrine
☐ Playwright August Strindberg's home is a museum.

islands woven tightly together by 30 bridges, trailing her fingers and toes in the waters of Lake Mälaren and the Baltic Sea. The lake, one of Sweden's largest, is half a meter higher than the sea, and a series of locks enables the city to hold on to its title of Sweden's second-largest port (Gothenburg is first). East of the city stretches an archipelago of 30,000 islands and beyond them, the Baltic.

Sweden is the fourth-largest country in Europe, encompassing about the same area as California (more than half covered by forest). Sweden and neighbors Norway and Finland dangle from the top of the world like a bunch of bananas.

Even though Sweden is at almost the same latitude as Greenland, the Swedes are blessed with a much milder climate thanks to the Gulf

Stream. In July, the average temperature is 64°F with 20 hours of daylight in which to enjoy it. In winter, temperatures drop only slightly below freezing, and the sun makes a brief appearance for a few short hours a day.

Agriculturally, Sweden is 80% self-sufficient, but the price of food is high. Farms are small and family-owned, selling mostly grains and meat through farm cooperatives.

CONSERVATION

In 1910 Sweden became the first European country to establish national parks in order to preserve some of its (and Europe's) remaining wilderness. Most of the parks are in the mountainous areas of Norrland, and there are numerous nature preserves and cultural heritage areas. Beaches are free to all, and anyone may hike through the forests and fields, picking berries and sniffing flowers at will. The waters around Stockholm have been made clean enough to swim in—40 years ago these same waters were polluted, but an enormous effort of environmental treatment and control has made it possible to take a dip in the downtown area.

PEOPLE

Sweden is a large European country, but its population would not fill the streets of Paris. There are some 8.5 million people (the same as New Jersey), and 1.5 million of them live in greater Stockholm. The people are homogeneous for the most part; even most of the 700,000 immigrants that have entered the country since World War II have come from other Scandinavian countries. The Sami people (Lapps) have lived in northern Sweden for thousands of years.

In Sweden a child is automatically born a Lutheran unless his or

---

IMPRESSIONS

The folk who live in Scandinavia
Are famous for their odd behavior.
They have the frigidest of climates
And avoid their bellicose fellow-primates.
Though salesmen cluster at the door,
They don't want anybody's war.
It isn't that they put on airs;
They merely mind their own affairs.
—ODGEN NASH
("FELLOW CREATURES, III: THE NORTHERNERS," IN *I'M A STRANGER HERE MYSELF,* 1938)

her parents request a waiver. Nine years of schooling are mandatory from age 7, and more than 90% of the population completes at least 2 more years of secondary education.

People in Stockholm enjoy a high standard of living, with almost no unemployment—only 1.4%. They work 9 to 5, and in summer knock off an hour early to enjoy the good weather. People get 5 weeks of paid vacation a year, but there's still a high rate of absenteeism—an average of 23 days a year.

In spring and summer, when the weather is good and the hours of sunlight long, it's hard to find the Swedes at home—unless it's their summer home. They head for the great outdoors and fishing, sailing, hiking, biking, and berry picking.

A little more than half the population live in apartments, which are increasingly hard to come by in Stockholm. People live simply and, by American standards, sparsely; their homes are clean, functional, and simple—just like the lines in typical Scandinavian furniture. The materials they choose are natural—pine, linen, cotton, glass, clay, and iron. The Swedes spend time at home and entertain there often.

Compared to the hurried, harried lifestyles of people in other parts of the world, the Swedes embrace balance and harmony and it shows in their demeanor—except when the subject of taxes comes up. People talk about taxes in Sweden the way folks in other countries discuss the weather, and with good reason. They pay anywhere from 50% to 72% of their income into the local and national kitties; a fixed percentage of their annual income—averaging out to about 40%—is paid out on the local level.

THE HEALTH-CARE SYSTEM

National health insurance takes care of Swedish citizens from the cradle to the grave. It covers hospital visits, lab fees, prescribed drugs, visits to doctors in public clinics, a part of fees to private doctors, and about 40% of dental costs. Parents are entitled to 18 months paid leave after the birth of a child; they may share it and take it at any time before the child is 8 years old.

In Sweden, life expectancy is high, the birth rate is low, and the country enjoys one of the lowest infant mortality rates in the world. People aged 65 receive a pension designed to provide two-thirds the income they received during their most profitable years of working.

HISTORY

Most of the earliest inhabitants of this region migrated north after the ice cap melted. They chose to live and work by the water, as do the inhabitants of Stockholm

DATELINE

- **1252** Stockholm becomes a city
- **1520** The Stock- *(continues)*

DATELINE

holm Bloodbath sees
the slaughter of 82
leading citizens

- **1523** Gustav Vasa
becomes king of
Sweden
- **1634** A new
Swedish constitution
is drawn up, and
Stockholm becomes
the national capital
- **1697** The royal
palace, "Three
Crowns," is de-
stroyed by fire
- **1850** The first
railway is inaugu-
rated
- **1877** The first
streetcar line goes
into service
- **1891** Skansen
opens
- **1901** The first
Nobel Prizes are
awarded in Stock-
holm
- **1912** Stockholm
hosts the Olympic
Games
- **1950** The first
subway line opens
- **1989** The Globe
Arena opens
- **1990** The new
Vasa Museum opens
in Djurgården
- **1991** The interna-
tional Stockholm
Water Prize is
awarded for the first
time

today. The early settlers lived by hunting
and fishing. As time passed, farming became
the way of life. The Viking Age, 800 to
1050, was marked by expansion eastward, in
some cases as far as the Black and Caspian
seas.

During the 13th century, Mälaren, an
arm of the Baltic Sea, became a lake; and in
1252 Birger Jarl founded Stockholm on its
shores (until there was a lake, no one
thought of putting a city here). The town
was founded on Stadsholmen (City Island),
now Gamla Stan, or the Old Town. Birger
Jarl's Tre Kronor (Three Crowns) castle
stood on the crown of the ridge, encircled
by a handful of houses and a wall. Anyone
wishing to enter or leave Lake Mälaren first
had to pay a customs duty, which brought in
plenty of revenue.

The road running along the wall of the
fledgling town is today Västerlånggatan, the
main shopping street in the Old Town. In
1697 the castle's tower was struck by light-
ning and the structure burned. The new
castle took almost 60 years to complete,
but the extra care paid off; it still stands
today.

THE STOCKHOLM BLOODBATH

In 1389, Sweden, Denmark, and Norway
were united into the Kalmar Union under
Danish Queen Margareta, but there was
great in-fighting and a struggle to maintain
autonomy, resulting ultimately in what became known as the Stockholm Bloodbath
(1520) and the dissolution of the union. At
the instigation of Danish King Christian II,
almost 90 leading Swedish citizens—the
opposition whom Christian conveniently
deemed "heretics"—were summoned to a
meeting at Stortorget in Gamla Stan and
executed by hanging or decapitation.

Christian thought his ruthlessness would
cow the opposition once and for all, but a
rebellion ensued and he was deposed. In

1523 Swedish nobleman Gustav Vasa became king of Sweden and Stockholm became the center of power for the country. Gustav Vasa reigned until 1560, heralding a period of growth for Sweden. The church was nationalized, with the king as its head, and the monarchy—which had been elective throughout the Middle Ages—became hereditary. The tradition of the Changing of the Guard was inaugurated during this time.

A TIME OF EXPANSION

By the 15th century, Stockholm filled the island of Gamla Stan and its population numbered 6,000. Great expansion, however, did not occur until the 1600s; at the end of the century the city's inhabitants numbered 50,000. Stockholm ranked as a major northern European power. The country's government, centered in Stockholm, set up a national road network and transportation system. The problems of the times were poverty, disease, and a high mortality rate.

Gustaf II Adolf (1611–32) became a strong monarch and military leader; and under his leadership, territory that had previously belonged to Denmark and Norway (a union at that time) was ceded to Sweden—this land now composes the country's southern and western regions. By 1658 Sweden had provinces on the southern and eastern shores of the Baltic Sea, as well as colonies in the West Indies and in North American, in what is now the state of Delaware.

Stockholm reigned as the country's major port until the 17th century, when Gothenburg was established on the west coast and served as the major center for exports. Stockholm, Gothenburg (now the country's second-largest city), and Malmö (at Sweden's southern tip and right across the Øresond from Copenhagen) are the country's major cities and are known as Sweden's three crowns.

CENTURIES OF CHANGE

After the Great Northern War from 1700 to 1721—with Denmark, Poland, and Russia pitted against her—Sweden lost much of her territory across the Baltic. Consequently, her size shrank to what now composes modern Sweden and Finland.

In 1809 King Gustav IV Adolf surrendered Finland to Russia. For many years Sweden had been ruled by power-hungry monarchs. But when Finland was lost, there was a coup d'état in which the king was deposed and a new constitution adopted.

Based on Montesquieu's theory of separation of powers, the Constitution of 1809 made the king sole ruler but stipulated that he share legislative power equally with Parliament. The constitution remained in force until 1974, making it then the second-oldest such document in the world after that of the United States.

In 1814 military force on Sweden's part "persuaded" Norway to form a union with Sweden. It lasted from 1814 to 1905, when it was dissolved amicably. That tussle in 1814 was to be the last for Sweden, which since then has firmly established itself as a peace-loving nation, following a foreign policy of nonalignment in peacetime and neutrality in wartime.

Between 1860 and 1880, as industry took hold, the city's population doubled—from 100,000 to 200,000. Folks living in the country could not support themselves, and for them migration was essential; many went to America. In fact, more than a million Swedes emigrated between 1866 and 1914, a notable loss for a country of only 5 million.

Industry developed rapidly from 1900 to 1930. Plans for a welfare society were laid in 1930 and put into action after World War II. In 1974 a new constitution relegated the king's duties to ceremonial functions only.

POLITICS

Sweden is a constitutional monarchy with a parliamentary form of government. Whereas the old constitution began with the words "The King alone shall govern the realm," its successor begins with "All public power in Sweden emanates from the people." The king is the head of state, and his duties include presiding over the opening session of Parliament each October; he receives heads of state and makes state visits abroad.

Parliament, called the Riksdag, has one chamber whose members are elected for 3-year terms. They select a prime minister, who chooses a cabinet, the members of which head a dozen or so ministries.

The country has half a dozen political parties, the strongest among them historically being the Social Democrats, which has ruled for 52 of the past 58 years. Other parties include the Moderates, the Liberals, the Center (formerly the Agrarian party), the Communists, and the Green party, the first new parliamentary party in nearly 70 years.

Sweden has a foreign policy of neutrality. It is not a member of Europe's Economic Community. The country has 12 nuclear reactors but voted in 1980 to phase out the use of nuclear power by the year 2010.

CARL XVI GUSTAF

Carl XVI Gustaf was born in 1946 and acceded to the throne of Sweden when he was 27. He went to boarding school in Sigtuna and studied at the universities in Uppsala and Stockholm. His particular interest is in nature conservation and environmental protection. His

IMPRESSIONS

The real Swedish gentleman is an honor to his country and to mankind.
—E. D. CLARKE
(*TRAVELS IN VARIOUS COUNTRIES*, 1824)

---

support of scouting has resulted in his becoming the honorary chairman of the World Organization of the Scout Movement. He is a sportsman, yachtsman, and skier.

He and his wife, Queen Silvia, married in 1976 and have three children—two daughters and a son. Queen Silvia grew up in São Paulo, the daughter of a Brazilian mother and West German father (a businessman who represented a Swedish firm in Brazil). When she was working as a Spanish interpreter at the Olympic Games in Munich in 1972, she met her future husband and Sweden's future king.

The eldest child of the king and queen is heir to the throne, regardless of sex. The present heir is Crown Princess Victoria, born to the royal couple in 1977.

SOME CULTURAL BACKGROUND

ART

Nature has inspired Swedish artists throughout history, as a visit to the National Museum or Thiel Gallery will quickly demonstrate. The French impressionists also influenced their Swedish counterparts; this is particularly apparent in the works of painters Ernst Josephson (1851–1906) and Carl Fredrik Hill (1849–1911).

Carl Larsson (1853–1919), who has been called a "stylized Swedish Norman Rockwell," celebrated Swedish family life in his paintings, using his wife and eight children as compelling subjects.

Anders Zorn (1860–1919) was known for his ability to capture light in his work, as well as for his soft, sensual nudes. This artist was also a world traveler who visited the United States six times and painted the portraits of American presidents Taft, Cleveland, and Theodore Roosevelt, as well as Andrew Carnegie.

Zorn and Larsson were contemporaries and friends (they died the same year), although Zorn came from a prosperous background and Larsson from one of poverty. The homes of both artists, Zorngården (the first home to have hot and cold running water in Sweden) and Sundborn, are open to the public; however, they require travel outside of Stockholm.

Carl Milles (1875–1955), Sweden's most widely acclaimed sculptor, lived in the United States from 1931 to 1951, as sculptor-in-residence and professor at Cranbrook Academy outside Detroit (where many of his works may be seen). Many of his sculptures can also be seen at Stockholm's Millesgården, a property that Milles and his wife, Olga, bought in 1906 and that he designed.

INVENTIONS

Sweden is known worldwide for it exports like Volvo, Electrolux, Orrefors and Kosta Boda crystal, crisp crackers (where would cheese be without them?), slotted cheese slicers, and Melita coffee filters. IKEA, the furniture manufacturer, is known around the world. Swedish design, perhaps more than any other, has great mass appeal.

The world owes other inventions to Swedes: consider self-adjust ball bearings, Styrofoam, the pacemaker, the refrigerator, the adjustable wrench, and the zipper. Swedes have also given the world the automatic lighthouse, the Saab turbo engine, the three-point car safety belt, the log cabin, Absolut vodka, and the Hasselblad camera, invented by Victor Hasselblad in 1942 and considered by many to be the finest in the world.

These inventions aren't all pleasant, however; Sweden is also credited with coming up with a contraption called the parking meter.

THE NOBEL PRIZE

In 1865 a Swedish inventor, Alfred Nobel, died and left his immense fortune—built chiefly on the discovery and manufacture of dynamite—to fund annual prizes for research. His relatives were not pleased with this and litigated the will for 5 years, to no avail. Today the coveted prizes, worth 2 million Kr ($36,363) are awarded by King Carl XVI Gustaf at a ceremony in Stockholm's Concert House (Konserthuset). The famous banquet (for 1,200 guests) is held in the Blue Hall in City Hall.

Nobel had stipulated that the prizes be awarded for the most valuable research during a 12-month period, but today that has changed to a body of work over a longer period of time. The prizes—for literature, economics, physics, chemistry, medicine—are awarded by academic committees for basic research, and the effect of it on daily life is not taken into consideration. The Nobel Peace Prize is awarded annually in Oslo by a Committee of the Norwegian parliament, as stipulated in Nobel's will.

Nobel, who lived in various European countries during his life, died in San Remo, Italy, and the town sends flowers for the Nobel Prize ceremonies every year.

Following the tradition of the Nobel Prizes, the Stockholm Water

Foundation inaugurated the Stockholm Water Prize in 1991; it goes to an individual or organization that has contributed substantially during the past 3 years to the conservation of the world's water resources. The prize, worth $150,000, is awarded in mid-August.

Stockholm sets a good example in water conservation. Thirty years ago, the water surrounding the city was polluted, but today, after an enormous effort of environmental treatment and control, people happily fish for salmon and perch. In 1973, for the first time in 40 years, the swimming areas in Stockholm were reopened to the public; one popular spot lies within sight of City Hall. Not a mean feat for a city of 1.5 million people.

2. FOOD & DRINK

MEALS & DINING CUSTOMS

Swedes, especially city dwellers, tend to eat a light breakfast before they dash off to work. And during this morning meal, they might burn a candle, in summer or especially during the long, dark winter days. Lunch is served around noon and is usually a hot meal.

Dinner used to be served early, around 5 or 6pm, but now is eaten later, though employees get off work at 5pm, and even earlier in summer—there tend to be no workaholics here. Restaurant kitchens are open until 10 or 11pm on weekdays, perhaps an hour later on weekends.

A main dish of meat or fish is usually accompanied by potatoes and other vegetables, with fruit and cheese for dessert. Coffee is served at the end of a meal more often than tea.

Coffee, in fact, is drunk all day long, and rarely is a visitor not welcomed with the words "Would you like a cup of coffee?"

IMPRESSIONS

Before they sit down to dinner, the company commonly take bread and butter, which they wash down with a glass of brandy; a fashion that prevails not only among persons of condition, but extends even to the ladies, as well as to the men. I must own that I cannot reconcile myself to a custom, which, though it doubtless originated from the extreme rigor of the climate, is only worthy of the Muscovites.
—SIR N. W. WRAXALL
(*A TOUR ROUND THE BALTIC*, 1775)

THE CUISINE

The Swedes are known for their *smörgås*, or open-face sandwich. Bread is embellished with everything from butter to cheese to ham, and is popular for breakfast, lunch, or a snack. Expand *smörgås* to *smörgåsbord* (or smorgasbord in English), and you have a delectable feast, a buffet meal that in olden times started out as a lavish hors d'oeuvre. Expect to find herring, salmon (including *gravad lax*, served with dill), and shrimp, followed by cold meats, pâtés, Swedish meatballs, and condiments.

Knowing the limitations of girth and pocketbook, Swedish restaurants will often serve a mini-smorgasbord, called *smör, ost och sill* (that means simply cheese, butter, and herring—something most of us can be quite content with).

Swedish *knäckebröd* (dry, crisp bread) has become a staple around the world. It is easily complemented with cheeses, of which Sweden produces a variety: from the stronger Västerbotten and Lagrad Svecia to the milder Herrgardsost and Grevé to a spiced cheese like *Kryddost*. Smoked reindeer meat is popular in the north but not so common in Stockholm restaurants.

Lingonberries and cloudberries are popular for jams and show up as readily with meat dishes as with pancakes. They also make delectable desserts.

At Christmastime, special foods are prepared, among them *lutfisk*, dried ling (fish) that has been soaked, then boiled and served with a béchamel sauce, mustard, boiled potatoes, and green peas. It is sometimes followed by a thick rice porridge served with cinnamon, sugar, and butter. An almond may be hidden in the porridge and whoever gets it will marry within the year. And everyone looks forward to munching on spicy, thin ginger cookies called *pepparkakor* in the shape of hearts. Saffron-flavored bread, called *lussekatter*, is served on Lucia Day, December 13.

DRINK

Drink in Sweden is more potent than it is varied. Aquavit (Absolut vodka) is known—and exported—the world over. The sale of alcohol is strictly controlled, and you will only find it in shops run by the state-run Systembolaget.

At Christmas, *glögg*—a hot cordial made with red wine, schnapps, and spices, and served with raisins and almonds—is a must. Originally, glögg was set afire; now it merely sets you afire. During the holidays, you might also be served *mumma*, a modern version of Viking mead, which is warming from the inside out.

Filmjolk is a fermented milk product and a Swedish specialty; it's a little like liquid yogurt. Regular milk is *mjolk* and low-fat is *lattmjolk*.

3. RECOMMENDED BOOKS, FILMS & RECORDINGS

BOOKS

Noted Swedish authors include Vilhelm Moberg, most famous for his works on the Swedish-American experience, especially *The Emigrants* (1950) but also *Unto a Good Land* (1953) and *The Last Letter Home* (1961); Per-Anders Fogelström, whose novels are set in Stockholm; and dramatist August Strindberg, famous for the realism of his plays. His work *The Red Room* (1879) depicts the bohemians of Stockholm.

Selma Lagerlöf, who won the Nobel Prize in Literature in 1909, penned works such as *The Story of Gösta Borling* (1894) and the children's classic *The Wonderful Adventures of Nils* (1906–07). Astrid Lindgren was the author of dozens of children's books and the creator of Pippi Longstocking.

The Old Town, by the writer/photographer team of Béatrice and Gösta Glase, is an excellent history of Stockholm's early days and a fine companion for a walk through Gamla Stan. Published by Trevi, it is available in bookstores in Stockholm and in the City Museum on Södermalm.

If you're interested in the Vikings, try Johannes Brondsted's *The Vikings* (Penguin Books, 1960), or Frans Bengtsson's *The Long Ships* (William Collins Sons, 1954), which is out of print but can be found in libraries.

FILMS

Sweden is most noted for two contemporary filmmakers: director Ingmar Bergman and cinematographer Sven Nykvist. In their long careers they have often been collaborators, in films that include *The Virgin Spring* (1960), *Cries and Whispers* (1972), *Scenes from a Marriage* (1973), and *Fanny and Alexander* (1983). Nykvist's other films include *Pretty Baby* (1978), *The Postman Always Rings Twice* (1981), and *The Unbearable Lightness of Being* (1988).

Good Evening, Mr. Wallenberg (1990), directed by Kjell Grede, is about Raoul Wallenberg, who accomplished the largest, most successful rescue of Jews during World War II, and who was taken prisoner by the Russians in Budapest and never released. *Hip, Hip Hurrah!* (1987), also directed by Grede, won the special grand prize at the Venice Film Festival as well as the prize for best cinematography.

Other Swedish films of note include *The Guardian Angel* (1990), directed by Suzanne Östen; *My Life as a Dog* (1985), directed by

Lasse Halström; *The Sacrifice* (1986), directed by Andrei Tarkovsky; and the children's films *Brenda Brave* and *Good Night Mr. Vagabond* (both 1988), directed by Daniel Bergman.

RECORDINGS

Opera fans can more than likely find cassettes and records (perhaps CDs) of Swedish opera stars such as soprano **Birgit Nilsson,** mezzo soprano **Elisabeth Söderström,** and tenor **Jussi Björling.** It's also possible to find recordings of the **Stockholm Symphony Orchestra** and the **Radio Symphonic Orchestra.** Baroque music by the **Drottningholm Ensemble** might be harder to find—outside Sweden, that is.

You certainly will have no problem finding cassettes and CD's of the well-known pop groups **ABBA** and **Roxette.**

It's possible to order some Swedish music through the **Swedish Book Nook,** P.O. Box 804, New York, NY 10028 (no telephone); write for a catalog. And once you're in Stockholm, visit the **Swedish Institute,** on the second floor of Sweden House, Hamngatan 27, off Kungstradgarden (tel. 08/789-2000). Here you'll find records, cassettes, and CD's, mainly of classical music.

FAMOUS STOCKHOLMERS

ABBA A Swedish pop music group that rocketed to fame in the 1970s, scoring four Top 10 hits in the United States: "Dancing Queen," "Knowing Me and Knowing You," "Take a Chance on Me," and "Fernando." ABBA are the initials of the four members' last names.

Ingmar Bergman (b. 1918) Film director/producer whose illustrious career began in the 1940s and has included *Wild Strawberries* (1957), *The Seventh Seal* (1957), *The Passion of Anna* (1969), *Cries and Whispers* (1972), *Scenes from a Marriage* (1973), *The Magic Flute* (1973), *Autumn Sonata* (1978), and *Fanny and Alexander* (1983). His work deals with complex moral, psychological, and metaphysical problems, and his characters are known for their brooding introversion and pessimism.

Ingrid Bergman (1915–82) Film actress who starred in such classics as *Intermezzo* (1939), *Casablanca* (1942), *Gaslight* (1944), *Notorious* (1946), *Anastasia* (1956), and *Autumn Sonata* (1978). During her career, she won three Oscars.

Bjorn Borg (b. 1956) Tennis player who was on the world-class circuits at 17 years of age. He won five consecutive Wimbledon singles titles beginning in 1976.

Curt Carlson (b. 1914) Born in Minneapolis to Swedish parents, he is chairman of the board of Carlson Companies, Inc., owner of the world's largest travel agency, among other holdings. He was made commander of the Royal Order of the North Star and of the Royal Order of Polar Star by King Carl XVI Gustaf in 1976 and 1988, respectively. Other honors include Swedish-American of the Year in 1981 and the Scandinavian-American Hall of Fame Award in 1989.

Stefan Edberg (b. 1966) Tennis player who won the Wimbledon singles title in 1988, the first Swede to do so since Bjorn Borg in 1980.

Greta Garbo (1905–90) Mysterious, charismatic film star known as the "Swedish Sphinx," who retired in 1941. Her film work began in Sweden in the 1920s; she came to the United States in 1925 and made 24 films, among them *Flesh and the Devil* (silent, 1927), *Queen Christina* (1933), *Anna Karenina* (1935), *Camille* (1936), and *Ninotchka* (1939).

Dag Hammarskjöld (1905–61) Secretary General of the United Nations from 1953 to his death, he presided over many Cold War disputes, notably the Suez Canal crisis. His sending of UN troops to the Belgian Congo (now Zaire) was bitterly denounced by the USSR. A collection of his speeches, *Servant of Peace,* was published in 1962, followed by *Markings* (1964) and *The Light and the Rock* (1966). After his death in a plane crash in the Congo, he was awarded the Nobel Peace Prize (1961).

Anders Hedberg (b. 1951) Outstanding player for the New York Rangers from 1978 to 1985.

Ingemar Johansson (b. 1932) Boxer who defeated Floyd Patterson in 1959 to become the world heavyweight boxing champion. (He was defeated by Patterson the following year.)

Jenny Lind (1820–87) Opera and concert singer, this soprano with a remarkable range was known as the "Swedish Nightingale." She successfully toured the United States from 1850 to 1852, and part of the trip was managed by P. T. Barnum.

Astrid Lindgren (b. 1907) Children's book writer and creator of Pippi Longstocking.

Vilhelm Moberg (1898–1973) Author who wrote about the province of Småland during the hard times of the mid-1800s and the people who emigrated from there to North America. Their struggles are captured in works such as *The Emigrants* (1950), *Unto a Good Land* (1953), and *The Last Letter Home* (1961).

Birgit Nilsson (b. 1921) Opera singer and recording star famous for her Wagner roles. She joined the Swedish Royal Opera in 1948, and debuted at New York's Metropolitan Opera in 1959, as Isolde.

Sven Nykvist (b. 1922) Cinematographer who had a long collaboration with Ingmar Bergman, beginning in 1960 with *The Virgin Spring.* He has also worked with Woody Allen, Paul Mazursky, and Norman Jewison, and others, on films that include

Pretty Baby (1978), *The Postman Always Rings Twice* (1981), and *The Unbearable Lightness of Being* (1988).

Olaf Palme   (1927–86) Prime minister of Sweden from 1969 to 1976 and from 1982 until his assassination by an unknown assailant in 1986. Educated in Sweden and the United States, this member of the Social Democratic party has been described as "upper class by birth and left wing by persuasion." As prime minister, he carried out constitutional reforms, turning the Riksdag into a single-chambered parliament and stripping the monarchy of its power.

Roxette   A pop duo with such international hits as "The Look," "Listen to Your Heart," "Dangerous," and "It Must Have Been Love," the theme from the 1990 movie *Pretty Woman*.

August Strindberg   (1849–1912) Playwright and novelist whose works include *Master Olaf* (1872), *The Red Room* (1879), *Miss Julie* (1888), *The Creditors* (1888), *To Damascus* (written in 1898 and 1904), *Dance with Death* (1901), *A Dream Play* (1902), and *The Spook Sonata* (1901). After publication of his short stories, *Marrying* (1883), he was unsuccessfully prosecuted for blasphemy. Although he is regarded as one of Sweden's greatest writers, his work is often criticized for its hostile attitude toward women.

Max von Sydow   (b. 1929) An actor who has appeared in many Ingmar Bergman films, including *The Seventh Seal* and *Wild Strawberries*. He portrayed Christ in *The Greatest Story Ever Told* in 1965. In 1988, he starred in the Oscar-winning Danish film *Pelle the Conqueror*.

Raoul Wallenberg   (1912–?) Businessman who at age 32 saved the lives of more than 100,000 Jews in Budapest, providing them with safe houses and false papers. He disappeared in the custody of the Soviets on January 17, 1945, and has never been seen since. Although the Soviet government claims that Wallenberg died of a heart attack in 1947, rumors persist that he is still alive in a Soviet prison camp, creating great public outcry and outrage that continues to this day.

CHAPTER 2

PLANNING A TRIP TO STOCKHOLM

Deciding where to go on vacation is easy compared to all the questions that come next, such as: How do I get there most economically? What will the trip cost overall? Where do I get up-to-date information before I go? Do I need to book anything ahead? This chapter addresses these and other issues that you should give some thought to as you begin to lay the groundwork for your trip. For instance, have you considered whether or not you need travel insurance, how much money to put into traveler's checks, whether or not to use a credit card, and, if you do, how to pay the monthly credit-card bills if you will be traveling for an extended period of time. Extra planning now can save hassles, time, and money later on.

1. INFORMATION, ENTRY REQUIREMENTS & MONEY

SOURCES OF INFORMATION

IN THE UNITED STATES

General information on Stockholm and Sweden may be obtained from the **Swedish Tourist Board,** 655 Third Avenue, 18th Floor, New York, NY 10017 (tel. 212/949-2333; fax 212/679-0835).

The **Swedish Information Service** can provide free pamphlets on Swedish culture, politics, and economics. It has offices in the following cities:

IMPRESSIONS

*The Swedes were in those days [1911], and still are, more
civilized than most Europeans. Their civilization was their
own . . . refreshingly alive and vigorous.*
—LEONARD WOOLF
(*BEGINNING AGAIN,* 1964)

New York—1 Dag Hammarskjöld Plaza, 45th Floor, New York,
10017-2201 (tel. 212/751-5900; fax 212/752-4789).
Los Angeles—10880 Wilshire Boulevard, Suite 505, Los Angeles,
CA 90024-4314 (tel. 213/470-2154; fax 213/475-4683).
San Francisco—120 Montgomery Street, Suite 2175, San Francis-
co, CA 94104 (tel. 415/788-2734; fax 415/982-7362).

Some fact sheets may also be obtained through the **Swedish
Consulate,** which has offices in Chicago, Houston, Los Angeles,
Minneapolis, New York, and San Francisco, and in Montréal and
Ottawa, Canada. Consult local phone books for addresses and
telephone numbers.

IN STOCKHOLM

There are several helpful sources of information in Stockholm. The
primary one is the **Stockholm Information Service,** on the
ground floor of Sweden House, Hamngatan 27 (tel. 08/789-20-00),
which answers questions and sells maps, guidebooks, and the
Stockholm Card. The **Swedish Institute** is also in Sweden House,
on the second floor (tel. 08/789-2000).

   Hotellcentralen, on the lower level of Central Station (tel.
08/24-08-80), makes hotel reservations, answers general questions,
and distributes free maps.

   The **SL Center,** on the lower level of Sergels Torg (tel.
08/23-60-00), provides information about local transportation and
sells a good transportation map as well as tickets for the system.

   (For more information, see "Tourist Information," in Section 1 of
Chapter 3.)

ENTRY REQUIREMENTS
DOCUMENTS

Citizens of the United States, Canada, Great Britain, New Zealand,
and Australia need only a valid passport to enter Sweden.

CUSTOMS

Sweden's enormously high taxes on alcohol are quite sobering. If you
want to tipple without taking out a mortgage, buy duty-free alcohol

before entering the country. Ditto for tobacco. Overseas visitors may import up to 1 liter (quart) of alcohol and 200 cigarettes.

MONEY

The Swedish currency is the **krona** (crown)—or **kronor (Kr)** in its plural form—made up of 100 **öre.** Bills come in denominations of 5, 10, 50, 100, 1,000, and 10,000 kronor. Coins are issued in 5, 10, and 50 öre, as well as 1, 2, and 5 kronor.

At this writing, $1 = approximately 5.50 Kr (or 1 Kr = 18¢). This rate of exchange was used to calculate the dollar values, rounded to the nearest nickel, given throughout the book. This rate fluctuates from time to time and may not be the same when you travel to Sweden, so please use the following table only as a general guide.

THE SWEDISH Kr & U.S. DOLLAR

Kr	U.S.	Kr	U.S.
1	.18	100	18.18
2	.36	125	22.72
3	.55	150	27.27
4	.73	175	31.82
5	.91	200	36.36
6	1.09	225	40.91
7	1.27	250	45.45
8	1.45	275	50.00
9	1.64	300	54.55
10	1.82	325	59.09
15	2.73	350	63.64
20	3.64	375	68.18
25	4.55	400	72.73
50	9.09	500	90.91

Internationally recognized traveler's checks and credit cards are accepted throughout Sweden.

WHAT THINGS COST IN STOCKHOLM	U.S. $
Taxi from Central Station to the Vasa Museum	11.80
T-Bana (subway) from the train station to an outlying neighborhood	1.80
Local telephone call	.35
Double room at the Grand Hotel (deluxe)	338.20
Double room at Östermalms Pensionat (moderate)	108.20

	U.S. $
Double room at Pensionat Oden (budget)	90.00
Lunch for one, without wine, at Alice B. (moderate)	8.20
Lunch for one, without wine, at Hötorgs Hallen (budget)	6.35
Dinner for one, without wine, at Le Bistrot de Wasahof (deluxe)	37.80
Dinner for one, without wine, at Slingerbulten (moderate)	29.10
Dinner for one, without wine, at Capri (budget)	12.70
Pint of beer in a bar	7.30
Coca-Cola in a cafe	2.90
Cup of coffee in a cafe	2.90
Roll of ASA 100 color film, 36 exposures	10.20
Admission to Drottningholm Palace	4.55
Movie ticket	10.90
Budget theater ticket	12.70

2. WHEN TO GO — CLIMATE, HOLIDAYS & EVENTS

CLIMATE

Most of Stockholm's special events and free outdoor concerts happen during summer, but spring and autumn—April, May, June, and September—are probably the prettiest times of year. And while citizens of many other countries think of winter as something to wait

IMPRESSIONS

Winter has decided to pass the summer here.
—SPANISH AMBASSADOR TO SWEDEN (1835)
(RECORDED BY HENRY WADSWORTH LONGFELLOW IN *SAMUEL LONGFELLOW, LIFE,* 1886)

out, the Swedes revel in this season. Cold weather sets in by October, and locals usually stay bundled up until April. January and February are the coldest months. Those in search of the Land of the Midnight Sun (in summer) or the shimmering Northern Lights will have to journey north of the Arctic Circle to Lapland to find them.

Stockholm's Average Daytime Temperature and Rainfall

	Jan	Feb	Mar	Apr	May	June	July	Aug	Sept	Oct	Nov	Dec
Temp. (°F)	27	26	31	40	50	59	64	62	54	45	37	32
Rainfall ″	1.7	1.1	1	1.2	1.3	1.7	2.4	3	2.4	1.9	2	1.9

HOLIDAYS

Sweden celebrates New Year's Day, Epiphany, Good Friday, Easter Sunday and Easter Monday, May Day, Ascension Day (Thurs of 6th week after Easter), Whitsunday and Whitmonday (also called Pentecost), Midsummer Day (weekend nearest to June 24), All Saints' Day (Sat following Oct 30), and Christmas (Dec 24–26).

STOCKHOLM CALENDAR OF EVENTS

JUNE

☐ **Stockholm Marathon.** Attracts thousands of local and world-class runners. Usually run in early June.

☐ **Midsummer Celebration.** Special events—most free—fill parks and other outdoor spaces. Weekend nearest June 24, the longest day of the year.

☐ ✪ **Stockholm Jazz and Blues Festival.** Programs for this annual event are available through the Stockholm Information Service. Held for 10 days from the last weekend of June through the first weekend of July.

JULY

☐ **Stockholm Jazz and Blues Festival.** See above.

☐ **Bellman Week.** Honors the 18th-century court poet Carl Michael Bellman. Revelers, many in period costume, celebrate with poetry and music at Gröna Lund and various other city parks. Mid-July.

AUGUST

☐ **Women's 10K Run.** Traditionally attracts more than 25,000 entrants. Schedule varies.

☐ ✪ **Stockholm Water Festival.** Established in 1991, it celebrates the element that makes Stockholm such a unique and lovely city—one in which swimming and fishing in the center of town are strong traditions. Festivities include live entertainment, music, dancing, sporting events, fireworks, and the awarding of the Stockholm Water Prize, a cash prize of $150,000, which goes to the individual or organization that has made an outstanding contribution to water conservation. Held for 10 days in early August.

SEPTEMBER

☐ **Sailboat Day.** The harbor becomes a showcase for boats of all shapes and sizes, from Sunfish to schooner. 1st week of September.

DECEMBER

☐ **Christmas Markets.** Stalls fill squares in Gamla Stan and Skansen, selling traditional foods, handcrafts, gifts, and other seasonal items. Held every Sunday beginning 4 weeks before the holiday.

☐ ✪ **Nobel Prizes.** Named after the Swedish inventor of dynamite, Alfred Nobel, the prizes are awarded for excellence in physics, chemistry, medicine, literature, and economics. The prizes were instituted in 1901. (The Nobel Peace Prize has been awarded annually in Oslo, as Nobel's will stipulated.) December 10.

☐ ✪ **Lucia** (the festival of lights). This is one of the most popular and colorful of all Swedish festivals, designed to brighten up a dark period. Celebrated on December 13, the shortest day (and longest night) of the year; festivities continue on the nearest Sunday, when a Lucia Queen is crowned with a headdress of candles during a ceremony in Skansen.

3. INSURANCE

Before leaving home, check to see if your health and property insurance coverage extends to Europe. If it doesn't, or the coverage is inadequate, consider purchasing short-term travel insurance that will cover medical and other emergencies.

Also check your homeowner's or renter's insurance for coverage for off-premises theft. Again, if you need more coverage, consider a short-term policy.

If you're traveling as part of a tour or have prepaid many of your vacation expenses, you may also want to purchase insurance that covers you if you have to cancel for any reason.

Your best bet may be to purchase a comprehensive travel policy that covers all catastrophes—big and small—such as trip cancellation, illness, emergency assistance, and lost luggage. A travel agent may sell you a policy (the price is low), or contact the following companies for more information:

Tele-Trip (Mutual of Omaha), 3201 Farnam Street, Omaha, NB 68131 (tel. toll free 800/228-9792).

Travel Guard International, 45 Clark Street, Stevens Point, WI 54482 (tel. toll free 800/826-1300).

Travel Insurance Pak, Travelers Insurance Co., One Tower Square, 15NB, Hartford, CT 06183-5040 (tel. toll free 800/243-3174).

For travel assistance that can bail you out with a loan of money in case of a serious midtrip medical emergency, contact:

Access America, 600 Third Avenue, New York, NY 10016 (tel. toll free 800/284-8300).

HealthCare Abroad (Medex), 243 Church Street NW, Suite 100D, Vienna, VA 22180 (tel. toll free 800/237/6615).

4. WHAT TO PACK

When traveling: Less is liberating. Never bring more luggage than you can carry. One bag (or backpack) is ideal. The bare-bones packing rule on garments is two: wash one, wear one.

CLOTHING

Even in summer, a sweater or light coat comes in handy in Stockholm, as temperatures drop at night and sometimes during the day, too. A raincoat with a removable lining is always practical in spring and autumn. Bring a heavy coat—and long johns—in winter, when temperatures hover around the freezing point. Jeans are popular with Swedes of all ages.

If you plan to travel with only a change or two of clothes, bring along some accessories to add diversity to your wardrobe: jewelry, a favorite hat, scarves, a vest, a tie.

In winter, pack boots suitable for walking in snow. Comfortable walking shoes are essential, especially in Gamla Stan (Old Town), where the streets are made of cobblestones; if you buy new shoes for the trip, be sure to break them in before you arrive.

Avoid taking along dry-clean-only apparel, because the cost in Stockholm is high—the equivalent of a good meal. Simple Laundromats are pricey, too, so choose articles that do not soil easily (or noticeably).

OTHER ITEMS

Bring your favorite brand of toiletries in sample sizes. Pack necessary items that aren't too heavy (tampons and condoms come to mind).

Bring a washcloth if you're in the habit of using one; hotels don't normally provide them.

Also pack converter and adapter plugs, a travel alarm, a small flashlight, copies of your passport and other documents for purposes of identification, prescriptions for drugs or eyeglasses, a Swiss Army knife, a collapsible umbrella, a sewing kit, and a sleep sheet if you plan to stay in hostels and don't have a sleeping bag.

5. TIPS FOR THE DISABLED, SENIORS, SINGLES, FAMILIES & STUDENTS

FOR THE DISABLED

Mobility International, P.O. Box 3551, Eugene, OR 97403 (tel. 503/343-1284), can provide information on travel, educational exchanges, and work camps.

The **Travel Information Service** of Moss Rehabilitation Hospital, 1200 West Tabor Road, Philadelphia, PA 19141-3099 (tel. 215/456-9600), is a center for treatment of the physically handicapped and has information on accessible hotels, restaurants, and attractions in Sweden—much of it supplied from firsthand reports.

Check your bookstore for *Access to the World: A Travel Guide for the Handicapped,* an informative 220-page book by Louise Weiss (Henry Holt).

FOR SENIORS

If you aren't already a member, consider joining the **American Association of Retired Persons (AARP),** 1909 K Street NW, Washington, DC 20049 (tel. 202/872-4700), which has a Purchase Privilege Program with discounts on lodging and car rentals abroad.

In Stockholm, visitors 65 years old and older receive discounts at the National and Modern Art museums, the Concert Hall, and the Royal Dramatic Theater, not to mention a 50% fare reduction on subways and buses. Keep that ID handy.

FOR SINGLE TRAVELERS

Servas and **Friends Overseas** are organizations that encourage peoples of different cultures to get together. You can contact them to arrange home stays or visits with Swedish members (see "Home Stays or Visits," below).

As far as lodging in Stockholm is concerned, the hostels are more centrally located than most hotels. Private homes charge lower rates than hotels and provide a wonderful opportunity to get to know your Swedish host.

FOR FAMILIES

Family Travel Times is an informative newsletter published 10 times a year for $35 by **Travel with Your Children (TWYCH),** 80 Eighth Avenue, New York, NY 10011 (212/206-0688); subscribers have access to a call-in service that answers questions about travel in specific countries.

Stockholm welcomes families to its parks and Skansen, an outdoor museum with Swedish cottages, cabins, and stone houses, and even a small zoo. There are free outdoor entertainment and activities in summer, and ice skating in the center of town in winter. Museums offer reduced admission for children. On public transportation, children between the ages of 5 and 12 pay half price; younger kids ride for free.

FOR STUDENTS

To enjoy special discounts while visiting Stockholm, flash the **International Student Identity Card** or, if you're of student age but not a student, the **International Youth Identity Card.** Both carry basic accident and sickness insurance coverage; have hotline access for medical, legal, and financial emergencies; and are available for $14 from the **Council on International Educational Exchange (CIEE),** 205 East 42nd Street, New York, NY 10017 (tel. 212/661-1450).

In Stockholm, a valid student ID provides discount admission at some museums, including the National and Modern Art museums, as well as the Royal Dramatic Theater, the Opera, and the Concert Hall. It almost costs less for students with ID to go to the theater here than it does to go to the cinema.

6. ALTERNATIVE/ADVENTURE TRAVEL

EDUCATIONAL/STUDY TRAVEL

The **Institute of International Education (IIE),** 809 United Nations Plaza, New York, NY 10017 (tel. 212/883-8200), and the **Council on International Educational Exchange** (address and phone under "For Students" in Section 5 of this chapter) provide free booklets and also sell books about study (and teaching) abroad.

Those 50 and older may partake of courses in Stockholm offered by **Interhostel,** University of New Hampshire, 6 Garrison Avenue, Durham, NH 03824 (tel. 603/862-1147, or toll free 800/733-9753). People 60 and older can contact **Elderhostel,** 75 Federal Street, Boston, MA 02110-1941 (tel. 617/426-7788).

HOME STAYS OR VISITS

Anyone would be enriched by a one-to-one exchange with a friendly citizen of Stockholm. To set up a visit, be it for afternoon tea or a shared excursion or a home stay, consider joining **Friends Overseas,** 68-04 Dartmouth Street, Forest Hills, NY 11375 (no phone). The organization has a successful American–Scandinavian People-to-People Program, and travelers pay $25 per visit to participate. For more information, send a stamped, business-size envelope to the above address.

Another organization, **Servas,** founded in Denmark in 1949, promotes peace and understanding by getting people of different cultures together. It has 60 hosts in Stockholm and environs, 345 hosts in Sweden all told. For more information, contact Servas at 11

John Street, Suite 706, New York, NY 10038-4009 (tel. 212/267-0252); the yearly membership is $45, with a $15 refundable deposit for host lists.

The **International Visitors Information Service,** 733 15th Street NW, Suite 300, Washington, DC 20005 (tel. 202/783-6540), lists organizations in 35 countries, including Sweden, in its *Meet the People* directory ($6.50).

WORK CAMPS

Participants in work camps arrange and pay for their own transportation, but work in exchange for room and board and the chance to perform socially significant tasks. Volunteers generally spend 2 to 3 weeks at a camp, and work a 5-day, 30-hour week in groups of 5 to 30 people. The minimum age to participate is 16 or 18; there is no maximum age. Most work camps take place from June through September.

To inquire about work camps in the Stockholm environs or in other parts of Sweden, contact **Volunteers for Peace International Workcamps,** 43 Tiffany Road, Belmont, VT 05730 (tel. 802/259-2759); **SCI International Voluntary Service,** c/o Innisfree Village, Route 2, Box 506, Crozet, VA 22932 (tel. 804/823-1826); and the **Council on International Educational Exchange,** 205 East 42nd Street, New York, NY 10017 (tel. 212/661-1414).

HOME EXCHANGES

If you'd like to swap your house or apartment for one in Stockholm, contact the **Vacation Exchange Club,** Box 820, Haleiwa, HI 96712 (tel. toll free 800/638-3841). The club's directory of more than 10,000 listings is published twice a year.

7. GETTING THERE

BY PLANE

THE MAJOR AIRLINES

Scandinavian Airlines (SAS) is the national carrier serving Sweden, Denmark, and Norway, with 60 international flights serving Stockholm daily. Its only direct flight is out of Newark Airport,

Newark, New Jersey, in the New York Metropolitan Area. However, SAS flights out of Los Angeles, Seattle, Chicago, and Toronto have a stopover in Copenhagen, with connecting flights to Stockholm.

TWA has direct flights from New York. **American Airlines** offers direct flights to Stockholm from Chicago. Airlines flying to Stockholm via other destinations include **Finnair** (via Helsinki), **Icelandair** (via Reykjavík), and **KLM** (via Amsterdam). For flights arriving from gateways outside North America, see "Arriving . . . By Plane" in Section 1 of Chapter 3).

International flights arrive at Arlanda Airport, 28 miles north of Stockholm. From New York the flight to Stockholm takes 8 hours; from London or Paris, 2.5 hours.

BEST-FOR-THE-BUDGET FARES

With an eye toward frugality, consider some alternative ways of getting to Stockholm by air.

Bucket Shops   Retail discount ticket agencies, or bucket shops, offer reductions of 20% to 30%, usually advertised in the travel sections of newspapers. These ads (the size of a postage stamp) simply list major European cities with a fare opposite each one. The tickets are restrictive, nontransferable, and nonrefundable except directly from the bucket shop.

Leading retail bucket shops selling air transportation to Sweden include **Access International, Inc.,** 101 West 31st Street, Suite 1104, New York, NY 10001 (tel. 212/465-0707, or toll free 800/827-3633); **Maharaja Travel, Inc.,** 395 Fifth Avenue, New York, NY 10016 (tel. 212/213-2020, or toll free 800/223-6862); **Sunline Express, Inc.,** 607 Market Street, San Francisco, CA 94105 (tel. 415/541-7800, or toll free 800/877-2111); and **Euro-Asia, Inc.,** 4203 East Indian School Road, Suite 210, Phoenix, AZ 85018 (tel. 602/955-2742, or toll free 800/525-3876), which also offers discount fares through travel agents.

"Budget" Airlines   Some of these companies have a reputation for consistently low fares, though—to be honest—in the last few years they have not been significantly lower than other carriers' fares. Still, be sure to check **Tower Air** (tel. 718/917-8500, or toll free 800/221-2500) or **Icelandair** (tel. toll free 800/223-5500).

Charter Flights   Drop by a travel agency and ask to see their most recent copy of *Jax Fax,* the monthly magazine of the air-chartering industry. This publication is useful for ferreting out dates, departure cities, and prices for charter transportation between North America and Europe.

When considering a charter flight, it's important to get complete price information. Some charter companies tack on high-season supplements, and other companies pass airport taxes directly on to the traveler. Make sure the flight you want is available for the date you need. If the base rate is from an eastern gateway city, the company may run connecting flights either as charters or in conjunction with regularly scheduled airlines from other U.S. cities. These flights are usually less expensive than independently booked flights, but you will pay an "add-on" fee.

Courier   If you're traveling alone and light—meaning one or two carry-on bags only—consider going as a courier. You get a greatly reduced fare, while the courier company gets your checked baggage space for its time-sensitive packages. The courier company offers only one seat a day, so if two of you are traveling together, try to arrange departures on two consecutive days. For more information, check the Yellow Pages of your telephone directory for courier services in your area, or contact **Now Voyager Freelance Couriers,** 74 Varick Street, Suite 307, New York, NY 10013 (tel. 212/431-1616).

SPECIAL FARES

Be sure to check out special fares offered by the carriers that fly to Stockholm on a regular basis, such as **SAS, Finnair, Icelandair, TWA,** and **American.** They are sure to have ads in the travel section of your local newspaper.

Early Fares   If time is on your side, take advantage of significantly reduced early fares, available to those who can commit to a particular flight 2 or 3 months in advance and can stay a minimum 7 days, a maximum 30 days. For example, in 1991, to those who could commit by April 8, SAS offered an early-bird fare of $598 round trip from New York to Stockholm in summer, $498 for flights made off-season (add an additional $100 for flights from Chicago and Minneapolis, $200 from the West Coast). Keep in mind that an "early fare" does not refer to the time the plane departs but to an advance booking.

Advance-Purchase Fares   These are also economical, although they are usually not as cheap as the early-bird specials. To obtain an advance-purchase fare, you usually have to purchase the ticket 14 to 30 days before departure, and stay in Europe at least 1 week but no longer than 3 weeks. Some advance-purchase fares don't even have the 2-week lead time; I've seen 1-day advance-purchase fares advertised. The fares are generally lower for midweek flights than for weekend ones. If you are a student or a senior citizen, always ask if a special discount applies to you.

REGULAR FARES

If advance-purchase fares aren't available, then you have to resort to regularly scheduled flights. Three fare possibilities are offered: **coach,** the most economical but also with the most cramped seats; **business class,** costlier but with more amenities and leg room (ask about an upgrade from coach; it may be less than you think and worth it for the lengthy transcontinental flight); and **first class,** costliest of the lot, short of flying the Concorde.

If you have to leave at a moment's notice, you may have to fly **standby,** taking whatever seat is available, be it coach, business class, or first class. No discount is offered for flying standby.

If you have to fly to or from Europe because of the death of a family member, some airlines offer a **bereavement fare.** It is not available through SAS, however.

 FROMMER'S SMART TRAVELER: AIRFARES

- The further ahead you plan and book your flight, the better you do on the fare. The airline is happy to have your money and will compensate you for your early commitment.
- If you plan to stay only a week (or less), look into specific land-air packages, which represent big savings—the equivalent of having hotel and breakfast thrown in for free.
- Comparison-shop all the airlines that fly to Stockholm. Fares to the three Scandinavian capitals are usually comparable.
- Inquire about early-bird, advance-purchase, and other discount fares, even if you have not seen them advertised.
- Keep calling airlines to check fares. Availability of inexpensive seats changes daily depending on the airline. As the departure date draws near, some airlines sell more seats at lower prices.
- Ask about senior or student discounts (SAS offers both).
- Consider flying in a shoulder (not quite peak) season, such as late September, October, late April, or early May, when fares are lower and the weather pleasant.
- The opening of borders in the European Community in 1992 may open the way for lowered fares within individual countries and within Europe itself. If you're pressed for time and have to fly from one city to another in Sweden, Scandinavia, or Europe, it's going to be more economical now than ever before.

BY TRAIN

Trains arrive frequently at Stockholm's **Central Station** from other countries and other parts of Sweden. There is a T-Bana (subway) stop here.

Usually, the most economical way to travel to Stockholm by train is via a **ScanRail** pass, valid for travel in Sweden, Denmark, and Norway. The pass costs $170 first class, $139 second class, for any 4 days of rail travel in a 15-day period.

If you're traveling to Stockholm from a part of Europe other than Scandinavia, consider purchasing a **Eurailpass,** which costs $230 for 5 days of travel within a 15-day period.

Both the ScanRail pass and the Eurailpass are available for longer periods than those mentioned here; both must be purchased in the United States prior to your trip. In many cases, the cost of either pass is less than what you would pay for individual fares for long-distance excursions.

For more information on the ScanRail pass and the Eurailpass, contact **Rail Europe,** Information Department, 230 Westchester Avenue, White Plains, NY 10604 (tel. 914/682-5172 in New York, New Jersey, Connecticut, or Canada; toll free 800/345-1990 in the rest of the U.S.).

BY BUS

Buses arrive in Stockholm at **Central Station,** on the ground level, whereas trains enter on the lower level, adjacent to the subway station.

BY CAR

Stockholm is 360 miles from Oslo, 400 miles from Copenhagen, and 205 miles from Gothenburg, Sweden's major port city.

Sweden stretches 2,000 kilometers (1,240 miles) from tip to toe. If you're traveling from northern Sweden, Kiruna or Luleå, for instance, you can stow your car on a train and leave the driving to someone else. The only drawback is that Gothenburg or Malmö is the closest you can get to Stockholm using this mode of transportation, so if you were planning an excursion to either of these two places, you may want to visit them first and then drive to Stockholm.

With the **SJ Motorail train,** you get to rest in a sleeping coach for one to three people or a couchette coach for up to six adults while your vehicle is transported in a container car. Motorail has a shop and a dining car, and breakfast is included in the cost of the ticket. For a couple, the price would start at about $400; children under 12 travel free when accompanied by an adult. For more information, contact a travel agent.

If you are driving from Finland, you will have to take the ferry from Turku (see "By Ship," below).

The speed limit in the inner cities of Sweden is 30 and 50kmh (19 and 31 m.p.h.), 70 to 90kmh (43 to 56 m.p.h.) on the highways, or 100kmh (62 m.p.h.) on the freeways. Speed limits are given in kilometers in Sweden, and 1 kilometer is equal to about 2/3 mile.

The wearing of seatbelts is obligatory, as is driving with your lights on at all times (low beams are sufficient during the day). The use of car lights has reduced accidents noticeably in Sweden. And be forewarned that Sweden has tough laws on drinking and driving.

Plan to carry an **international driver's license** in Sweden, available for $10 through any branch of **American Automobile Association (AAA),** along with your own driver's license. If you are a member of AAA, find out how to contact those Swedish auto associations that are affiliated with AAA—they may be able to help you with maps, highway routing, and Customs information, but usually do not provide emergency road assistance. AAA headquarters is at 1000 AAA Drive, Heathrow, FL 32746-5063 (tel. 407/444-8000).

BY SHIP

Ferry service began in the Baltic Sea as recently as 1959, and today there are about 10 shipping companies plying the waters. **Viking Line,** the largest, with more than 50% of the market, has daily service between Stockholm and Helsinki. Contact Viking Line, c/o Euro Cruises, 303 West 13th Street, New York, NY 10014 (tel. 212/691-2099 in New York, or toll free 800/688-EURO in the U.S. and Canada; fax 212/366-4747).

Silja Line is the next largest operator in Baltic waters, offering service between Stockholm and Helsinki, and Stockholm and Turku, Finland, with departures in either direction. The company's new ship, the *Helsinki,* travels between its namesake and Stockholm and features an open, central atrium five decks high and 140 meters (455 ft.) long, giving passengers the chance to commune with both sea and sky throughout the voyage. The atrium has a glass roof and large side windows, and provides a view for the usually deprived inside cabins. For more information, contact Silja Line, 505 Fifth Avenue, New York, NY 10017 (tel. 212/986-2711 in New York, or toll free 800/323-7436; fax 212/983-1275).

Scandinavian Seaways offers overnight service between Amsterdam and Gothenburg and between Harwich, England, and Gothenburg. The trips take about 24 and 27 hours, respectively, and there are excellent train and bus connections to Stockholm from Gothenburg. Contact the company through its North American representative, **DFDS Seaways,** Crown Place, Suite 212, 6499

NW Ninth Avenue, Fort Lauderdale, FL 33309 (tel. toll free 800/533-3755 in the U.S. and Canada; fax 305/491-7958). DFDS Seaways can also book rail tickets, Avis Rent-a-Car vehicles, and Best Western hotels, which offer economical Hotel Cheques in Sweden and other countries.

BY CRUISE LINER

Cruise liners visit Stockholm in summer as part of their 2-week and longer northern European itineraries. Among those docking at Stockholm Harbor are Cunard's **Vistafjord,** which pays a visit in August, and the **Royal Viking Sun,** which calls three times in July and once in early August. For more information, contact a travel agent or the Swedish Tourist Board.

PACKAGE TOURS

Fly-drive holidays and Scandinavia Super Savers are available May through September from **SAS Viking Vacations,** 270 Madison Avenue, New York, NY 10016 (tel. toll free 800/344-9099; fax 212/779-8944). City package tours of 1 to 30 days are offered year round by **Scantours,** 1535 Sixth Street, Suite 205, Santa Monica, CA 90401 (tel. toll free 800/223-SCAN; fax 213/395-2013) and **SuperCities** 7855 Haskell Avenue, Van Nuys, CA 91406 (tel. toll free 800/888-8685); and from April through October (3 or 6 days only) by **American Express Vacations,** 300 Pinnacle Way, Norcross, GA 30071 (tel. 404/368-5100; fax 404/368-5184).

    Scandinavian Express offers a budget tour of the Scandinavian capitals (Stockholm, Copenhagen, and Oslo). The company is represented in the United States by **Scanworld,** 12444 Ventura Boulevard, Studio City, CA 91604 (tel. toll free 800/622-5355; Canadians call collect 818/506-4114).

8. ENJOYING STOCKHOLM ON A BUDGET

THE $50-A-DAY BUDGET

The Scandinavian countries are some of the most expensive in Europe, particularly Sweden and Norway. And out of a travel budget that has to be carefully portioned out, figure that the largest chunk will go for lodging. If you don't stay in youth hostels or rent a room in a private home, you have to resign yourself to spending $50 a day here.

For two people traveling together, which is the most economical way to do it, figure *each* person will spend roughly $35 for a room in a private home, and $15.45 to $20 a day in a hostel. If you choose to stay in a hotel room with a bath, figure on spending $45 per person a day and adjust your budget upward. Factor in another $15 or $20 each for meals; that allows a minuscule amount for alcohol but plenty for one substantial meal, one lighter one, and as many snacks as you like. Breakfast is included in the price of some hotel rooms, and this helps keep eating-out expenses down.

What you spend on activities, entertainment, and transportation is up to you. It's not figured into the dollar-a-day total here. Fortunately, Stockholm encourages walking, which keeps transportation expenses low—although the city is too spread out for you to walk everywhere. The **Stockholm Card** (see "Tourist Information" in Section 1 of Chapter 3) is truly a good deal and covers bus and subway fares, sightseeing tours by bus, and admission to most of the city's attractions. The **Stimulating Stockholm** program also offers excellent values (see "Tourist Information" in Section 1 of Chapter 3).

Much of the entertainment in summer is outdoors and as free as the crisp, clear air.

To stick to your $50-a-day (or less) goal, be creative and selective. The tips below will help.

SAVING MONEY ON ACCOMMODATIONS

Accommodations will undoubtedly be your biggest expense in Stockholm. Youth hostels are cheapest, and in Stockholm two of them are located right downtown—almost as nicely situated as the illustrious Grand Hotel itself. Your next option is lodging in a private home, which affords more privacy than a hostel, with the added pleasure of your getting to know your Swedish host. Unlike those of many cities, Stockholm's least expensive hotels are not clustered around the train station, but are scattered throughout the city. This is only a minor disadvantage, since they are a quick subway ride from the train station or the center of town. As in other Scandinavian cities, upscale hotels in Stockholm drop their rates in summer, when business travel drops off. Still, for budget travelers, they remain pricey.

If you like interacting with local folks and don't mind swapping some touring time for chatting time, home stays are a wonderful alternative to hotels or hostels. While you don't pay anything for the experience, you do have the responsibility to arrive when you say you will, keep respectable hours, be a thoughtful guest, and spend time conversing with your host.

SAVING MONEY ON MEALS

Plan on spending at least $10 to $12 on one hearty meal daily, and eat smaller ones, or snacks, throughout the day to tide you over. Make lunch rather than dinner your big meal of the day, since it costs less. You cannot cook in the city's hostels, but you can use the kitchen in some of the private homes (see individual listings in Chapter 4). Buy and eat lots of fresh fruit, which is both satisfying and healthful. If you stay in a hotel, choose one that includes breakfast in the room rate (Swedish breakfasts tend to be simple, not sumptuous, so don't expect it to tide you over until dinner).

SAVING MONEY ON SIGHTSEEING & OTHER ENTERTAINMENT

It's easy to save money on entertainment in Stockholm, where part of the fun is simply strolling along the inviting streets, especially in Gamla Stan (Old Town), and soaking up the ambience, architecture, and history. The benefits are twofold: Walking is free and it's good exercise. There are free concerts in summer, and the Stockholm Card, good for 2 or 3 days, provides phenomenal savings year round (see "Tourist Information" in Section 1 of Chapter 3).

SAVING MONEY ON SHOPPING

Shopping tends to be expensive in Stockholm, but if you indulge in a gift or souvenir or two, you can expect impressive value and craftmanship for your money, especially when it comes to crystal and clothing (furniture, too, if you want it enough to lug it home or have it shipped).

If you buy goods for more than 100 Kr ($18.20), ask the shopkeeper for a **Tax-Free Shopping Cheque** (valid for 1 month) in order to get back the VAT (Value-Added Tax) when you leave the country (see Section 1 of Chapter 8).

SAVING MONEY ON SERVICES & OTHER TRANSACTIONS

You'll get a better exchange rate if you change traveler's checks at banks rather than at hotels or in shops. If you use your credit card, *you'll receive the going exchange rate when the bill arrives at the headquarters of your credit card company,* be it 2 weeks or 2 months after you made the purchase. (This works in your favor if the dollar grows stronger by the day, against you if the dollar grows weaker.)

The least expensive way to place phone calls from abroad is by pay phone, never from the phone in your hotel room. Call collect or use your calling card or credit card, which some readers claim is the best bargain of all.

Tipping is the exception, never the rule, in Stockholm; a tip is already included when you receive your bill at a restaurant. Taxi drivers, however, expect an additional 10% of the fare on the meter.

GETTING TO KNOW STOCKHOLM

On a map Stockholm appears disjointedly dotted across numerous islands almost as far north as Siberia, and this may lead you to believe mistakenly that Stockholm is cold and remote. When you're there, however, you find that it is something else altogether: the most beautiful capital in Scandinavia and one of the loveliest cities in the world. At first glance, the Swedish people may appear cool and distant, but when you get to know them, their warmth and openness are disarming.

1. ORIENTATION

ARRIVING

BY PLANE

Airport Stockholm's **Arlanda Airport** is 45 kilometers (28 miles) north of town. Before you reach Customs, you can change money in the baggage claim area at a **bank** offering reasonable rates. Adjacent red telephones offer local calls of up to 3 minutes for 2 Kr (35¢).

IMPRESSIONS

It is not a city at all . . . simply a rather large village, set in the middle of some forests and some lakes. You wonder what it thinks it is doing there, looking so important.
—INGMAR BERGMAN
(IN AN INTERVIEW WITH JAMES BALDWIN, 1960)

Beyond Customs are representatives from most of the major **car-rental companies.** Downstairs, the **left luggage office** stows bags for 20 Kr ($3.65) per item per day. The office never closes (tel. 797-60-80).

From the airport's **information office,** which is open 24 hours, you can pick up a helpful city map. Six dayrooms are available should you need to rest.

Airlines Stockholm is served by a number of airlines, most frequently by **SAS,** which has 60 international flights into Arlanda Airport daily. Also calling on a regular basis are **Finnair, Icelandair,** and **American.**

Getting to & from the Airport Four rainbow-striped **buses** (tel. 23-60-00) leave the airport from in front of the Arrival Hall every 10 minutes from 5:45am to 10:05pm. Take the one designated "Stockholm City" to City Terminal. It costs 40 Kr ($7.30) for everyone over 16 (those younger, accompanied by a parent, ride for free), and the journey takes 40 minutes. **Taxis** are available at the airport (if you don't see one, call 0760-18040), but the ride into town will run you 400 Kr ($72.70).

BY TRAIN

Central Station, Stockholm's train station on Vasagatan, looks more like an international airport than the airport does. It is not in the heart of town, and from here you'll most likely have to take the subway to your hotel or hostel. The station has three levels, and can be confusing in its enormity. (Buses arrive and depart here, too.) Here's a quick walk-through the main areas:

Trains arrive on the **lower level,** where you can connect directly to Stockholm's handy subway system; look for the sign "Tunnelbana." The lower level is also home to the tourist office and Hotellcentralen, where you can book hotel rooms (see introduction to Chapter 4 for more details). Look for the illuminated green "i" pointing the way. Baggage carts and photo machines are across the corridor from Hotellcentralen.

Lockers are available for 10, 15, or 20 Kr ($1.80, $2.70, or $3.65) on the lower level, but it is much safer to make use of the left luggage office on the **ground level** upstairs, which charges 40 Kr ($7.30) per bag per day, 20 Kr ($3.65) per backpack. It's open daily from 6am to 10pm.

Train tickets are sold on the ground level. Windows 1–10 are for foreign travel; windows 11–26, for domestic. The ground level also has telephones, train information (SI Information), and a currency-exchange office, which is open daily from 8am to 9pm; look for the big yellow-and-black sign.

On the **lowest level** (below the lower level—it is confusing), you'll find a large market, along with clean bathrooms—there's a 2 Kr (35¢) charge to use them—that have large showers, which cost 17 Kr ($3.10). An attendant is on duty.

BY BUS

Buses, including airport buses, arrive at the ground level of Central Station (see "By Train," above, for more logistics).

BY CAR

From the north, you are likely to drive into Stockholm via Uppsala or Västerås, from the southwest via Gothenburg, and from the south via Norrköping. Roads are well marked, and traffic is moderate to sparse in most areas.

TOURIST INFORMATION

Your first stop in Stockholm should be **Sweden House (Sverige huset)**, Hamngatan 27, off Kungsträdgården. On the ground floor, you'll find the **Stockholm Information Service** (tel. 789-2000), the country's main tourist office, which will reserve a hotel room for you for a service charge of 20 Kr ($3.65), plus an 8% deposit on the room. Be sure to get a free copy of *Stockholm This Week* for its lists of special and free events and its good map. The Stockholm Card, described below, may be purchased here, along with city-tour and archipelago-excursion tickets, stamps, posters, cards, and gift items. Their 202-page *Discover Stockholm* book for 35 Kr ($6.35) is a good investment; a map of Stockholm and surrounding areas costs 10 Kr ($1.80). There is a convenient but locked bathroom on the premises, and you have to ask someone to buzz you into it. The Stockholm Information Service is open mid-June to August 31, Monday through Friday from 9am to 6pm, and on Saturday and Sunday from 9am to 5pm; the rest of the year, Monday through Friday from 9am to 5pm, and on Saturday and Sunday from 9am to 2pm.

The **Swedish Institute,** conveniently located on the second floor of Sweden House, provides free pamphlets on the Swedish economy, culture, and politics. The institute also sells a wide variety of English-language and photography books about Sweden, along with children's books, art books, records, cassettes, and CDs. It's open Monday through Friday from 9am to 6pm in summer, until 5pm in winter.

Information Stockholm is located in the House of Culture (Kulturhuset), Sergels Torg 3 (tel. 700-01-00). Local art exhibitions and cultural performances are often held here for free and are open to the public. For information on these events, the Stockholm city government, or Swedish society in general, visit the information desk on the second floor. Information Stockholm is open on Tuesday through Friday from 11am to 6pm, and on Saturday from 11am to 2pm.

Recorded announcements in English of events for the day may be heard by dialing 22-18-40.

THE STOCKHOLM CARD

On days when you do heavy sightseeing, the Stockholm Card will prove one of the city's most outstanding values. Just 190 Kr ($34.55) for 2 days, and 265 Kr ($48.20) for 3 days, buys you unlimited rides on the public transportation network, admission to most of the city's museums, free guided city sightseeing tours, and a guidebook to Stockholm. The Stockholm Card provides a half-price discount on boat sightseeing, as well as a one-way ticket to Drottningholm Palace. The card may be purchased at the tourist information counter at Sweden House and at Hotellcentralen at Central Station; it is valid for one adult and two children under the age of 18.

OTHER DISCOUNTS

If you visit off-season (from October to April), you can take advantage of the special activities and discounts offered through the **Stimulating Stockholm** program. Some of the best deals focus on exercise: ice skating, cross-country skiing, horseback riding, and fitness and Tai Chi classes. Ask for the brochure and more details at the Stockholm Information Service counter in Sweden House.

CITY LAYOUT

MAIN ARTERIES & STREETS

Drottninggatan, the major pedestrian shopping street, runs approximately north–south and bisects the neighborhood of

---

IMPRESSIONS

I have seen no town with whose situation I was so much struck as with that of Stockholm, for its singular and romantic scenery.
—WILLIAM COXE
(*TRAVELS INTO POLAND, RUSSIA, SWEDEN, ETC.*, 1792)

Norrmalm. Along this thoroughfare are the important squares of **Sergels Torg** (the pulsing heart of the city center) and **Hötorget,** homes to the Åhléns and PUB department stores, respectively.

Branching east from Sergels Torg is **Hamngatan,** a short street lined with chain-store outlets, the NK department store (Sweden's largest and most elegant), Sweden House (home of the Stockholm Information Service), and **Kungsträdgården,** which is half park, half street, and the location of many free outdoor events in summer, as well as ice skating in winter.

Birger Jarlsgatan, a few blocks east of Kungsträdgården, is filled with interesting shops and cafes as far as Sturegallerian, the trendy new shopping gallery at **Stureplan.** It's also the address of the Royal Dramatic Theater and the American Express office.

Strandvägen is the wide harbor-hugging thoroughfare lined with stately buildings; it leads from downtown Stockholm (pick it up just east of the Royal Dramatic Theater) to Djurgården and slightly beyond.

FINDING AN ADDRESS

When trying to find an address, be aware that the odd numbers on one side of the street often do not match the even numbers on the opposite side. For instance, on a block on Sveavägen, buildings numbered 55 through 63 are opposite buildings numbered 82 through 90.

NEIGHBORHOODS IN BRIEF

Try to picture the city as the group of islands it actually is—even though, for all intents and purposes, bridges and tunnels connect them as one. Fortunately for visitors, of the thousands of islands that make up the Stockholm archipelago, the important tourist destinations are closely clustered near Stockholm.

Norrmalm The heart of modern Stockholm, it is actually on the mainland, in the northernmost part of the city center. Here you will arrive at the train station, visit the Stockholm Information Service in Sweden House, shop in the major stores, and probably find a hotel.

Kungsholmen Due west of Norrmalm, Kungsholmen is home to Stockholm's striking City Hall, where the Nobel Prize banquet is held annually.

Gamla Stan [Old Town] It is clustered on a small island that takes center stage on most maps of Stockholm, and rightly so. Quaint buildings, cobblestoned streets, narrow alleyways, and unique shops provide a welcome counterpoint to Norrmalm's big-city landscape. In olden days, fast currents on either side of the island

forced sea merchants to portage their goods to vessels waiting on the other side. The paths they pounded are now the oldest extant streets in Stockholm and well worth exploring—in rubber-soled shoes.

Södermalm South of Gamla Stan, this is an area that up until about 12 years ago was considered the "bad" side of town. Today, as the city gentrifies, people clamor to live here. Rents have rocketed, and chic restaurants, bars, and clubs have moved in. Thankfully, you can still find budget hotels and pleasant private rooms in Södermalm, along with an enchanting view from the cliffs overlooking Stockholm Harbor or from the Katarina Elevator.

Skeppsholmen   Due east of Gamla Stan, across a narrow channel, lies this tiny teardrop-shaped island that is home to the

Museum of Modern Art and two ideally located youth hostels, one of which is a sleek three-masted schooner. The quiet lanes on the island are perfect for strolling or jogging.

Djurgården [Deer Park]   Farther east still is Stockholm's tour de force, magnificent Djurgården, where you'll find a number of the city's top sights. The envy of any lumberjack, this shady neck of land, with lush oak groves, has been protected for centuries by the government, which has historically maintained the area as a grazing ground for the king's deer (though you're more likely to see young lovers strolling arm-in-arm than deer today). The Vasa Museum and the massive outdoor Skansen folk museum are the island's top draws, though several other good museums are located here, too.

STREET MAPS

It's not necessary to buy a street map of Stockholm, as you'll find a reliable one at the back of the free tourist board publication *Stockholm This Week*. Larger and equally good maps—also free— are published by, and available through, the NK department store and the Hard Rock Cafe.

See also "Finding an Address" above.

2. GETTING AROUND

BY PUBLIC TRANSPORTATION

SL, Stockholm's efficient city transportation network, provides both bus and subway service. Subways are popularly called T-Bana, short for Tunnelbana. Fare is charged according to a zone system; the farther you go, the more you pay. Most destinations in central Stockholm will cost 12 Kr ($2.20), payable at the subway entrance or to the bus driver.

In addition to the **Stockholm Card** (described above under "Tourist Information"), other transportation discounts are available. SL sells two **day passes:** a 1-day unlimited-use pass for central Stockholm and the Djurgården ferries for 30 Kr ($5.45), and a 1-day pass that encompasses all of greater Stockholm for 50 Kr ($10). Kids pay half price for either. In fact, anyone under 18 and senior citizens may buy half-price tickets for all forms of public transportation.

The **SL Center,** on the lower level of Sergels Torg, sells tickets and a good map to the system. The staff will answer all your questions on local transportation; their office is open Monday through Thursday from 8:30am to 6:30pm, on Friday from 8:30am to

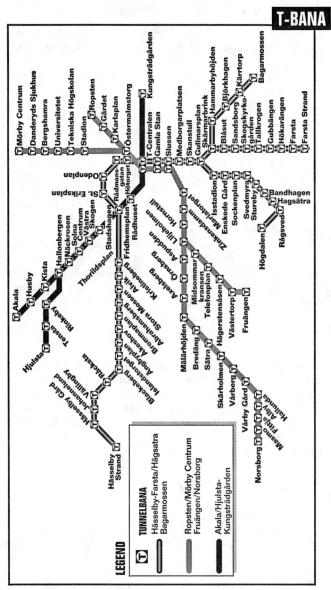

LEGEND

T **TUNNELBANA**

Hässelby-Farsta/Hägsatra
Bagarmossen

Ropsten/Mörby Centrum
Fruängen/Norsborg

Akala/Hjulsta-
Kungsträdgården

5:30pm, and on Saturday from 10am to 3pm (tel. 23-60-00 daily from 7am to 9pm).

BY SUBWAY

Stockholm is blessed with a fast and far-reaching subway system, the **T-Bana,** but you'll probably never have to take it for more than a few stops. The color-coded maps on station walls and printed in most tourist publications make the T-Bana easy to use. Timetables for each train are also posted.

Escalators in some of the city's 99 subway stations are steep enough to rival London's. More than half the stops are distinctive for the permanent artwork and other decoration they display; especially eye-catching are Kungsträdgården, T-Centralen, and Slussen.

A single ticket costs 10 Kr ($1.80) and is good for 1 hour (use it as much as you can). A 24-hour unlimited-use card costs 28 Kr ($5.10); for 55 Kr ($10), you get a strip of 15 coupons. Whether you are paying with cash or using a strip ticket, pass through the gate and tell the person in the ticket booth where you are going. He or she will either ask for your fare or stamp your ticket. Unlimited transportation is included in the cost of the Stockholm Card. If you have one, flash it and you'll be waved through.

Note: Most subway stops have several exits, all well marked; save yourself time (and avoid walking several blocks out of your way) by checking your map and choosing the exit closest to your destination. The SL runs shorter trains during the evenings, when there are fewer riders, so stand toward the center of the platform for boarding.

BY BUS

Buses run where subways don't (and where they do, too), comprehensively covering the city. Enter through the front door and pay the driver, or have your strip ticket stamped. If you plan on making extensive use of buses, buy a transport map from the Stockholm Information Service or the SL Center (see addresses above). Many buses depart from Norrmalmstorg, which is catercorner to Kungsträdgården, and 2 blocks from Sweden House.

BY FERRY

From May to September, ferries ply the waters between Gamla Stan and Djurgården, providing the best link between these two heavily visited areas. In summer, boats depart daily every 20 minutes from 9am to 1am; otherwise, Monday through Friday from 9am to 5pm, and on Saturday and Sunday from 9am to 6pm. The ride costs 12 Kr ($2.20) for adults, 6 Kr ($1.10) for seniors and for kids from age 7 to 18; children under age 7 ride free.

BY TAXI

Just a word of advice on taxis: Beware! The meter starts at 24 Kr ($4.35), and a short ride can easily come to 60 Kr ($10.90). You may order a cab by phone (tel. 15-00-00). Avoid gypsy cabs, and always take one with a yellow license plate with a "T" at the end of the number.

BY CAR

Unless you are planning an extended trip outside Stockholm, you will find that keeping a car in the city is more trouble than it's worth. Once you tally the cost of a car rental and gas, and compare it to the cost of public transportation, you're likely to leave the driving to someone else.

If you belong to the **American Automobile Association (AAA),** 1000 AAA Drive, Heathrow, FL 32746-5063 (tel. 407/444-8000), find out which Swedish auto associations are affiliated with AAA, as these organizations may be of help to you by supplying maps, highway routing, and Customs information (but not emergency road assistance).

RENTALS

If you choose to rent a car, you'll find that most major American car-rental firms have counters at the airport and offices in Stockholm. For example, downtown, you will find **Avis,** Sveavägen 61 (tel. 34-99-10); **Budget,** Sveavägen 153-155 (tel. 33-43-83); and **Hertz,** Vasagatan 24 (tel. 24-07-20); along with **Europcar,** Birger Jarlsgatan 59 (tel. 23-10-70).

Local companies, which may be cheaper, are listed under "Biluthyrning" in the Stockholm phone book and occasionally in the "Shopping" section of *Stockholm This Week.*

Car-rental companies have a minimum-age requirement, which ranges from 20 to 25, depending on the company; the driver must have a valid driver's license, along with an international driver's license. Figure on spending about $105 a day, including insurance, VAT, and unlimited mileage; or $275 a week, plus VAT (25%) and insurance. When booking an air or rail ticket, it's sometimes possible to book a rental car as well in a fly-drive package.

PARKING

Parking is permitted in most areas. In the inner city, where it is more difficult, there are various large parking garages marked with the international symbol for parking, "P." Garages in the downtown area charge a lower fee between 6pm and midnight. There are also many parking lots, some of which are located on the outskirts of town near the T-Bana stations. Most charge a fee.

Streets are cleaned once a week, and parking is not permitted during that time; check the sign at each street corner for specifics. Some parking spots are reserved, designated by a dark-blue sign with white lettering.

DRIVING RULES

The wearing of seatbelts is obligatory. This includes passengers riding in the backseat if the car is equipped with seatbelts in the back. Small children must be seated in a baby car-seat; if the car-seat is in the front seat, it must be placed with its back to the dashboard.

Headlights must be used while driving at all times; parking lights are sufficient during the day (this has resulted in a decreased number of accidents).

Swedes have driven on the right side of the road only since 1967.

BY BICYCLE

Bicycling is particularly recommended for exploring the island of Djurgården. **Skepp o Hoj** rents bikes starting at about 55 Kr ($10) a day, from April through September (tel. 660-57-57). Skepp o Hoj is conveniently located on Djurgården, right after you cross the bridge onto the island.

FAST FACTS: STOCKHOLM

Airport   Stockholm's **Arlanda Airport** is 28 miles (45 km) north of town. See "Arriving . . . By Plane" in Section 1 of this chapter for more information.

American Express   The Stockholm office gets a gold star from travelers for friendliness and helpfulness. Located catercorner from the Royal Dramatic Theater at Birger Jarlsgatan 1 (tel. 14-39-81), the American Express office will exchange money and hold or forward mail (see "Mail," below). There is an automatic cash machine on the premises. The office is open Monday through Friday from 9am to 5pm, and on Saturday from 10am to 1pm. For 24-hour refund assistance, call 020-795-155.

Area Code   For Stockholm it is **08** (all numbers in this book assume that prefix, unless otherwise noted). When dialing from the United States, drop the **0**.

Baby-Sitters   To find a baby-sitter, ask the proprietor of your hotel or guesthouse for a recommendation, or consult the baby-sitter column of the daily newspaper *Dagens Nyheter*. Deluxe hotels usually keep a list of baby-sitters, and even if you aren't a guest, they'll probably share it with you.

Banks   Most banks are open Monday through Friday from 9:30am to 3pm. Some in central Stockholm are open Monday through Thursday only, from 9am to 5:30pm.

Bookstores   The best prices and a large selection of books are found at **Akademi Bokhandeln,** Regeringsgatan and Mäster Samuelsgatan (tel. 21-15-90), open Monday through Friday from 9:30am to 6pm, and on Saturday from 10am to 2pm (3pm in winter). Check out the bargain bin. Fiction is upstairs, in the back on the left. Large and impressive, **Hedengrens Bokhandel,** Stureplan 4 in Sturegallerian (tel. 611-5132), has big travel and fiction sections downstairs. You'll also find a nice architecture section. They have a smaller shop a block away, at Kungsgatan 4, that sells discounted books in English. A novel by Graham Greene or Marguerite Duras will probably run you 65 to 85 Kr ($11.80 to $15.45) wherever you buy it.

Business Hours   **Shops** are usually open Monday through Friday from 9:30am to 1pm. Larger stores may maintain longer hours Monday through Saturday, and may open on Sunday as well. Most **offices** are open Monday through Friday only, from 9am to 5pm.

Car Rental   See "By Car" in Section 2 of this chapter.

Climate   See "Climate" in Section 2 of Chapter 2.

Currency   You'll pay your way in Stockholm in Swedish **kronor (Kr),** or crowns (singular, krona), sometimes abbreviated SEK, which are divided into 100 **öre.** Bills come in denominations of 5, 10, 50, 100, 1,000, and 10,000 kronor. Coins are issued in 5, 10, and 40 öre, as well as 1, 2, and 5 kronor. For money exchange, see "Banks," above, and "Currency Exchange," below. See also the currency equivalency chart "The Swedish Kr and U.S. Dollar" ("Money," Chapter 2, Section 1); this chart should be used as a general guide only as exchange rates fluctuate.

Currency Exchange   Rates of exchange are posted at banks and in daily newspapers. They do not vary from bank to bank, although commissions do. These fees can be sky high, usually 30 or 35 Kr ($5.45 or $6.35) per traveler's check or cash transaction; however, you may exchange up to six checks per one transaction. So to avoid repeating the costly commission fees, it's a good idea to change as much money as you think you will need at one time.

Competitive rates are also offered by many post offices, including the main branch, which keeps long hours (see "Mail," below, for details). The exchange window at the train station also keeps long hours, from 8am to 9pm daily. Conveniently located American Express (see above) also has an exchange window and there's no service charge.

Dentists   Emergency dental care is available at **St. Eriks Hospital,** Fleminggatan 22 (tel. 54-11-17, or 44-92-00 after 9pm). Regular hospital hours for walk-ins are 8am to 7pm. At other times, call first.

Doctors Normally, emergency medical care is provided by the hospital closest to the area in which you are staying. **Medical Care Information** (tel. 44-92-00) can provide you with this information, as well as with advice regarding injuries. **Cityakuten,** a privately run infirmary at Holländargatan 3 (tel. 11-71-77), can also provide help.

Documents Required See "Entry Requirements" in Section 1 of Chapter 2.

Driving Rules See "By Car" in Section 2 of this chapter.

Drugstores See "Pharmacy" below.

Electricity 220 volts are used in Sweden, so you'll need a converter, as well as an adapter with two thin round prongs (as opposed to the flat prongs required in the United States and Canada).

Embassies The **U.S. Embassy** is at Strandvägen 101 (tel. 783-53-00); the **Canadian Embassy,** at Tegelbacken 4 (tel. 23-79-20); the **Embassy of the United Kingdom,** at Skarpögatan 6-8 (tel. 667-01-40); the **Australian Embassy,** at Sergels Torg 12 (tel. 613-29-00). **New Zealand** does not maintain an embassy in Stockholm; inquiries should be made through the Australian Embassy.

Emergencies For the **police,** the **fire department,** or **ambulance service,** call **90-000.**

Etiquette Keep in mind that Swedes tend to be more subdued in public than Americans. Try eating the way Swedes do, with a knife and fork (in left hand) in unison, rather than with the fork only. Watch them for cues, and you may get the hang of it.

Eyeglasses Almost every street has an "Optiker," which can repair or replace broken glasses (though not while you wait). **Tollare,** Hamngatan 37, in the center of the Gallerian shopping mall (tel. 20-13-33), has friendly service and a good selection of contemporary styles. It's open Monday through Friday from 9:30am to 6:30pm, on Saturday from 9:30am to 4pm, and on Sunday from noon to 4pm. Or try **NK Optik,** in the NK department store at Hamngatan 18-20 (tel. 762-87-78); it's open Monday through Friday from 10am to 6pm, and on Saturday from 10am to 3pm.

Hair Stylists A wash and cut will run 250 to 285 Kr ($45.45 to $51.80). Try **Yvon Holm** in the Sturegallerian shopping center (tel. 611-80-81); **Hairteam** in the Gallerian shopping center on Hamngatan (tel. 20-06-40); or **Fatale,** Norrlandsgatan 22 (tel. 611-54-54).

Holidays See "When to Go" in Chapter 2.

Hospitals For the hospital closest to you, phone **Medical Care Information** (tel. 44-92-00), or visit **Cityakutan,** Holländargatan 3 (tel. 11-71-77), a privately run infirmary.

Information See "Sources of Information" in Section 1 of Chapter 2 and "Tourist Information" in Section 1 of this chapter.

Language Refer to Appendix A. Or pick up Berlitz's pocket-size *Swedish for Travellers,* available in the travel section of most bookstores in the United States and in Stockholm. The handy guide is color-coded according to subject; it contains useful phrases for travelers, along with their pronunciations spelled out phonetically. Most people in Stockholm speak English, so you may get little use out of it. The glossary of food terms should come in handy in restaurants.

Laundry/Dry Cleaning   A few of the hotels listed in the next chapter offer laundry facilities. There is a **self-service laundry** at Västmannagatan 61, where for 50 Kr ($9.10) you can wash and dry 5 kilos (11 lbs.) of dirty clothes. The price includes washing powder, and you should plan to arrive 2 hours before closing; it's open Monday through Friday from 9am to 6pm (except between 1 and 2pm), and on Saturday from 10am to 2pm.

In addition, **HB Wash,** Luntmakargatan 64 (tel. 673-58-80), charges 80 Kr ($14.55) to wash and dry 5 kilos (11 lbs.) of laundry. They also do dry cleaning, but be aware that this service is notoriously pricey in Stockholm, to the tune of 66 Kr ($12) to clean slacks, a jacket, or a skirt, or 29 Kr ($5.30) for a shirt. HB is open Monday through Friday only, from 8:30am to 5:30pm.

Library   The **Municipal Library (Stadsbiblioteket),** Sveavägen 73 (tel. 23-66-00), has foreign periodicals on file. It is open Monday through Thursday from 10am to 8:30pm, on Friday from 10am to 6pm, and on Saturday and Sunday from noon to 4pm.

Liquor Laws   Alcohol is state-managed and sold in special liquor stores, which are usually open Monday through Friday from 9am to 6pm. You have to be 20 years old to purchase beer, wine, or liquor. Bars and restaurants serve alcohol from noon on and stay open to the early morning hours of 1 to 4am, some even later.

Lost Property   If you lost property on a **bus** or the **T-Bana,** check at the **SL office** at the Rådmansgatan stop (tel. 736-07-80). If you lost property on a **train,** check the **lost-and-found office** on the lower concourse of Central Station (tel. 762-20-00). If you lost property **elsewhere,** check with the **police lost-and-found office,** Tjärhovsgatan 21 (tel. 769-30-75).

Luggage Storage/Lockers   Luggage storage is provided at Arlanda Airport, and at the train station (see "Arriving . . . By Train" in Section 1 of this chapter).

Mail   Located diagonally across from Central Station, the main **Stockholm Post Office,** Vasagatan 28-34 (tel. 781-20-20), is open Monday through Friday from 8am to 8pm, and on Saturday from 9am to 3pm. Most local post offices are open Monday through Friday from 9am to 6pm, and on Saturday from 9am to 1pm. A centrally located post office at Regeringsgatan 65 (tel. 781-21-38)—only a couple of blocks from Sweden House and the NK department store—is open Monday through Friday from 8:30am to 6:30pm, and on Saturday from 10am to 1pm.

You can receive mail either at the main post office (marked "Poste Restante" with a "Hold until . . ." date) or at **American Express.** The mail service at American Express, Birger Jarlsgatan 1 (tel. 14-39-81), is free; two mail deliveries are made here daily, at 9:30am and at 3pm. Amex charges 15 Kr ($2.70) to forward mail; it's open Monday through Friday from 9am to 5pm, and on Saturday from 10am to 1pm.

Maps   See "Maps" in Section 1 of this chapter.

Money   See "Money" in Section 1 of Chapter 2. See also "Currency" and "Currency Exchange," above in this section.

Newspapers/Magazines   There are no English-language newspapers or magazines printed in Sweden. The *International Herald-Tribune* and *USA Today* are available at newsstands all around town and in most hotel news shops. British newspapers and the latest American and British magazines are also readily available. A broad selection of periodicals can be found at the service-center level of the **NK** department store and at the **International Press Center,** Regeringsgatan 12 (tel. 21-22-64), open Monday through Friday from 10am to 6:30pm, and on Saturday from 10am to 4pm.

Expressen, a liberal tabloid, and *Dagens Nyheter,* an independent newspaper, are Stockholm's largest selling dailies. Even if you can't read Swedish, you might be interested in scanning their advertising and nightlife pages.

Finally, foreign periodicals can be read (free) at the **House of Culture (Kulturhuset),** Sergels Torg 3 (see "Tourist Information" in Section 1 of this chapter), and at the **Municipal Library (Stadsbiblioteket),** listed above under "Library."

Pharmacy   For 24-hour service, go to **C. W. Scheele,** Klarabergsgatan 62 (tel. 24-82-80).

Photographic Needs   Film can be purchased and processed in shops on almost every street in the city center, especially in the major tourist areas. One-hour film processing is available at Central Station. For camera supplies, try **Hasselblads Foto,** Hamngatan 16 (tel. 21-40-42), open Monday through Friday 9:30am to 6pm, and on Saturday from 10am to 2pm. Department stores offer two-for-the-price-of-one specials on film during the summer.

Police   For emergencies, dial 90-000. For other matters, contact **Police headquarters (Polishuset),** Agnegatan 33-37 (tel. 769-30-00). One conveniently located precinct office is inside Central Station.

Post Office   Stockholm's main post office is at Vasagatan 28–34, diagonally across from Central Station. It's open Monday through Friday from 8am to 8pm, and on Saturday from 9am to 3pm. See "Mail," above.

Radio   There are only three FM radio stations in the Stockholm area, all state-run. Radio Stockholm relays the BBC World Service news Monday through Friday at 7pm on 103.3 FM. Radio

Sweden International, at 89.6 FM, broadcasts programs in English daily at 1:30pm, 4pm, 5:30pm, 7pm, 9pm, 3am, and 4:30am (call 784-72-38 for time changes). If you have an AM receiver, you may even hear broadcasts from Moscow and beyond.

Religious Services   Some 92% of Swedes belong to the Church of Sweden, a Protestant church inspired by Martin Luther and other Continental reformers. The **Stockholm Cathedral (Storkyrkan)**, Old Town (tel. 723-30-00), consecrated in 1279, holds regular services and is open to the public. Prostestant Sunday services in English are held at 9am at **Immanuel Church**, Kungstensgatan 17 (tel. 15-12-25). Other houses of worship include **Stockholm Cathedral (Roman Catholic)**, Folkungagatan 46 (tel. 40-00-81), and the modern, centrally located **Santa Eugenia Catholic church**, Kungsträdgårdsgatan 12 (tel. 10-00-70); the **Islamic Congregation**, Torsgatan 48A, ground floor (tel. 31-61-75); and the **Great Synagogue (Jewish-Conservative)**, Wahrendorffsgatan 3A (tel. 23-51-60).

Restrooms   Public restrooms are called *toalett* in Swedish: *herrtoalett* for men, *damtoalett* for women. They are available in Central Station and most fast-food restaurants. There is also a restroom on the ground floor of Sweden House, Hamngatan 27. It's locked, so ask someone at the Stockholm Information Service counter to buzz you in.

Safety   As large cities go, Stockholm is a safe haven. Take the usual precautions you would in any unfamiliar city: Stay alert and be conscious of your immediate surroundings; wear a moneybelt and keep a special eye on cameras, purses, and wallets—items that say "come hither" to pickpockets and other scofflaws. Be particularly careful on dimly lit streets and in parks at dusk, which you should avoid after dark.

Shoe Repair   There is while-you-wait shoe repair at **Mister Minit**, in the NK department store at Hamngatan 18-20 (tel. 762-85-83); it's open Monday through Friday from 10am to 6pm, and on Saturday from 10am to 3pm.

Sundries   For items as various as washcloths to detergent, visit **Oskerson's**, Kungsgatan 70-72 (tel. 11-01-83) or Hornsgatan 74 (tel. 84-40-65). A large shop that sells toiletries is located in Slussen beside the post office and opposite the subway station.

Taxes   Sweden is legendary for its painfully high income taxes—as much as 72% in the top bracket. Fortunately, visitors to Stockholm need only concern themselves with the 24.6% VAT (Value-Added Tax) applied to most goods and services. In actuality, you won't really have to worry about this, either, as the VAT is already added to the prices in stores, to those on restaurant menus, and to hotel tariffs. Many stores offer non-Scandinavian tourists the opportunity to recover the VAT on purchases over 200 Kr ($36.35). See Section 1 of Chapter 8 for details.

Taxis As mentioned above under "Getting Around," taxis in Stockholm are expensive. Even if you are traveling in a group of four and split the fare, it's still costly. The meter begins at 24 Kr ($4.35) and rises rapidly; a 10% tip is customary. Advance reservations may be made by dialing 15-00-00, for which there should be no extra charge.

Telephone, Telex, and Fax The area code for Stockholm is 08, and all numbers listed in this chapter (and others) assume that prefix, unless otherwise noted. Public phones are fairly straightforward. **Local calls** cost 2 Kr (36¢) for the first few minutes, and an additional krona for every 2 minutes after that (depending on distance). Phones accept 1 Kr, 5 Kr, and 50 öre coins.

The easiest way to call the United States is via **AT&T's USA Direct** service. If you have an **AT&T Calling Card,** or call collect, you can reach an **American operator** from any phone by calling 020-795-611. Deposit 2 Kr before dialing. Alternatively, **international calls** may be made from the **Telecommunications Office** in Central Station (tel. 10-64-39), open Monday through Friday from 8am to 8pm, and on Saturday from 9am to 10pm. The **Telecenter,** Skeppsbron 2 (tel. 780-78-90), just across the bridge in Old Town, also offers a number of telecommunications services. A call to the United States from here costs 11.50 Kr ($2.09) per minute daily from 10pm to 10am; from 10am to 10pm, rates rise to 15 Kr ($2.70) per minute.

The Telecenter will also hold **telexes** for you sent via no. 17019. Ask the sender to specify "Hold for [your name]" on the telex; or if the sender includes your local telephone number, the staff at the Telecenter will contact you when it arrives. The Telecenter charges 15 Kr ($2.70) per page to send a fax. Open daily from 8am to 9pm. Credit cards are accepted (AE, DC, EU, MC).

Television The public-service Swedish Broadcasting Corporation operates two television networks **(TV1 and TV2).** Programs range from children's shows to news, documentaries, and entertainment; there are no commercials. Foreign programming is available through cable and satellite. **TV3,** a commercial satellite channel, is broadcast from England and aimed at the Scandinavian countries. A new Swedish channel, **TV4,** started operation in 1990.

Time There is a 6-hour time difference between Sweden and the East Coast of the United States (Eastern Standard Time). Sweden observes Daylight Saving Time, starting about a week before the United States does.

Tipping A 10% to 15% service charge is routinely included in hotel and restaurant charges; further tipping is unnecessary unless service is extraordinary. Taxi drivers expect an additional 10%, and cloakroom attendants get 4 to 6 Kr (about a dollar).

Transit Information Call 23-60-00, daily from 7am to 9pm.

Useful Telephone Numbers For the **police,** the **fire department,** or **ambulance service,** call **90-000.** For the **hospital** closest to you, call **Medical Care Information** at **44-92-00.** To reach an **American operator** from any phone, dial **020-795-611.** You can reach **Alcoholics Anonymous** at **42-26-09** for information about meetings in English. For tourist information, call the **Stockholm Information Service** at **789-2000.**

3. NETWORKS & RESOURCES

FOR STUDENTS

Stockholms Universitets Studentkar (Student Center) (tel. 16-02-60 or 16-30-97; ask for "Information Allhuset") is found in the university's Allhuset building. The center houses two restaurants and a travel agency, and the organization sponsors frequent parties (usually every Wednesday and every other Monday and Friday). Several student hangouts surround the campus, but the building's own restaurant, Allhuset Lantis, is probably the cheapest. A meal here costs as little as 30 Kr ($5.45). Lantis is open Monday through Thursday from 11am to 6pm, and on Friday from 11am to 2pm. To get to the Student Center, exit the T-Bana at Universitetet (five stops from Central Station) and walk straight ahead for a couple of minutes.

Note: The above facilities are closed during summer break, from the end of May until the beginning of September.

SFS Resebyra, Kungsgatan 4 (tel. 23-45-15), is the place for low-cost student and youth rail and air tickets. It's open Monday through Friday from 9:30am to 5pm. The office is 1 block from Birger Jarlsgatan at Stureplan.

Transalpino, Birger Jarlsgatan 13 (tel. 679-98-70), offers discount plane tickets and specially priced train fares for students of all ages with valid ID. It's open Monday through Friday from 10am to 5pm.

IMPRESSIONS

The most liberal hospitality to strangers is the distinguishing characteristic of the Swedes: it is a virtue which they sometimes carry to such an excess, as even to prove troublesome to travelers from the delay it occasions.
—E. D. CLARKE
(*TRAVELS IN VARIOUS COUNTRIES,* 1824)

FOR GAY MEN & LESBIANS

Local gays gather at **RFSL-Huset,** Sveavägen 57 (tel. 736-02-12). This large building is headquarters for most of Stockholm's gay organizations and also houses a restaurant (Alice B), a cafe (Cafe Timmy), a disco (Pride), and a bookstore (Bokhandeln Rosa Rummet).

Alice B. (tel. 31-55-33) is a smart eatery with an adventurous dinner menu slightly above our budget (lunch, however, is within range). Reservations are suggested for evenings, when it tends to get crowded. A tasty 45 Kr ($8.20) lunch special is served to a sparser crowd Monday through Friday from 11am to 3pm. Dinner is served on Monday, Tuesday, and Thursday from 5pm to midnight; and on Wednesday, Friday, and Saturday from 5pm to 12:30am (for more information, see "Extra-Special Lunch Specials" in Section 2 of Chapter 5).

Cafe Timmy (tel. 31-55-33) features a bistro menu, small tables surrounding a fountain, and occasional live music. With a marble floor and a high-ceilinged skylight, this is a good place for people watching; it's open on Monday, Tuesday, and Thursday from 11am to midnight, on Wednesday and Friday from 11am to 3am, and on Saturday from 4pm to 3am.

Pride (tel. 31-55-33), a small disco, is in the back of the building (see "Dance Clubs/Discos" in Section 2 of Chapter 9).

Bokhandeln Rosa Rummet (Pink Room Bookstore) (tel. 736-02-15) has a good selection of Swedish- and English-language books on current gay issues, as well as T-shirts and postcards. It's open Monday through Friday from 6 to 9pm, and on Saturday and Sunday from 3 to 6pm.

To get to the RFSL-Huset complex, take the T-Bana to Radmansgatan, or bus no. 52 to Sveavägen. Look for the green-and-pink neon sign that says "Pride" out front.

STOCKHOLM ACCOMMODATIONS

Stockholm offers several accommodations alternatives for the budget traveler. The most economical is staying in a centrally located hostel, followed closely by a stay in a private home, many of which offer use of the kitchen for free. Budget hotels, which will still run you $73 and up for a double room, are mostly in Norrmalm and accessible by public transportation. Room rates include tax, which is a whopping 25%. Breakfast is included only where noted in individual listings.

Hotellcentralen (tel. 08/24-08-80), on the lower level of Central Station, sometimes offers reduced-price hotel rooms for same-day occupancy during slow periods. Of course, not all hotels offer discounted rooms, but those that do usually lower their rates later in the day. There is a 24 Kr ($4.35) booking fee. The office is open May through September, daily from 8am to 9pm; April and October, daily from 8am to 5pm; and November through March, Monday through Friday from 8:30am to 5pm.

Hotelljänst, Vasagatan 15-17, 4th floor, 11120 Stockholm (tel. 08/10-44-67; fax 08/21-37-16), regularly rents 50 private rooms and charges excellent set rates of 200 Kr ($36.35) single and 300 Kr ($54.55) double. There is no service fee, but a minimum 2-night stay is required. Private rooms must be reserved 10 days in advance.

The office sometimes offers select hotel rooms at discounts of up to 50% in summer. This can add up to high-quality singles for about 400 Kr ($72.70), and doubles for 660 Kr ($109.10). You may reserve hotel rooms anytime in advance. The office, which has a 24-hour

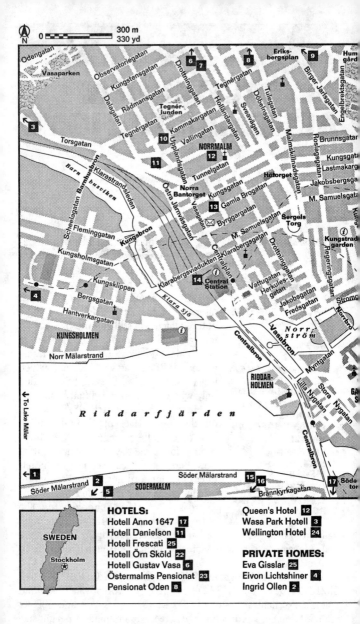

answering machine, is located 2 long blocks from Central Station; turn right when you get off the elevator. It's open Monday through Thursday from 9am to noon and then from 1 to 5pm (to 4pm on Friday).

Another way to save money on lodging is to participate in a

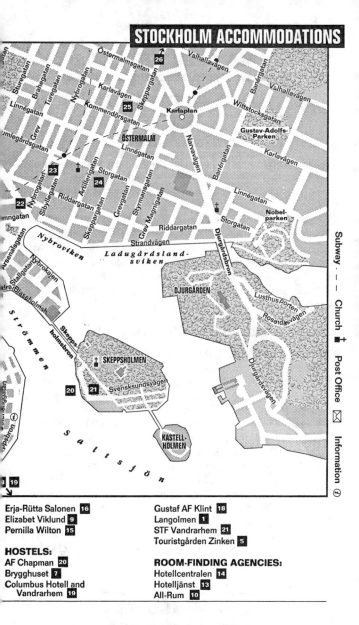

Subway - - - Church ⬛ Post Office ⊠ Information ⓘ

Erja-Rütta Salonen **16**
Elizabet Viklund **9**
Pernilla Wilton **15**

HOSTELS:
AF Chapman **20**
Brygghuset **7**
Columbus Hotell and
    Vandrarhem **19**

Gustaf AF Klint **18**
Langolmen **1**
STF Vandrarhem **21**
Touristgården Zinken **5**

ROOM-FINDING AGENCIES:
Hotellcentralen **14**
Hotelljänst **13**
All-Rum **10**

program such as **Best Western Hotel Cheque Scandinavia,
Scandinavian Bonus Pass,** or **Scandic Hotel Cheque.** These
programs allow you to purchase coupons in the United States for $25
to $35 each that are good for a night's lodging each in participating
hotels. For more information, check with a travel agent.

1. BARGAIN SINGLES & DOUBLES FOR LESS THAN 250 KR ($40.45)

NORRMALM

HOTELL ÖRN SKÖLD, Nybrogatan 6, S-11434 Stockholm. Tel. 08/667-02-85. 2 single rms (neither with bath). **T-Bana:** Line 13, 14, or 15 to Östermalmstorg, just 1 stop from Central Station.

$ Rates: 225 Kr ($40.90) single, AE, DC, EU, MC, V.

Not fancy, these two small, basic, bathless singles rent on a first-come, first-served basis for the lowest rates in town. There's barely room for you and your bag, and the toilet and shower are a walk away. Still, the location is central and a block from the American Express office. Other rooms in this upscale hotel are definitely outside budget range.

OUTSIDE THE CENTER

HOTELL   FRESCATI, Professorslingan 13-15. Tel. 08/19-94- 34 (make advance reservations through Hotell Domus, Körsbärsvägen 1, S-11489 Stockholm; tel. 08/16-01-95; fax 08/16-62-24). 120 rms (all with bath). **T-Bana:** Universitetet; then walk for 15 to 20 minutes or take bus no. 603.

$ Rates: About 200 Kr ($36.35) single; about 120 Kr ($21.80) per person double or triple. Sheets 45 Kr ($8.20) extra; towels 20 Kr ($3.65). Breakfast 45 Kr ($8.20) extra; dinner about 60 Kr ($10.90). No credit cards. **Open:** June–Aug only.

From September through May, the Frescati is home to students from several local universities. Come summer, it metamorphoses into a hotel and one of the best deals in town for wayfarers of all ages. The red-brick complex also houses a restaurant, a supermarket, and various shops—and imposes no curfew. It's outside the city center but pleasantly situated beside a stream and walking trails, and near inexpensive shops and cafes.

2. A DOUBLE FOR 400 KR ($72.70)

NORRMALM

HOTELL GUSTAV VASA, Västmannagatan 61, S-11325

Stockholm. Tel. 08/34-38-01 or 34-13-20. 33 rms (11 with bath). TEL **T-Bana:** Odenplan.

$ **Rates** (including Continental breakfast): 33 Kr ($60) single without bath, 420 Kr ($76.35) single with bath; 400 Kr ($72.70) double without bath, 520 Kr ($94.55) double with bath; 200 Kr ($36.35) per person in family rooms for 3 or 4 people. AE, DC, EU, MC, V.

⭐ The Gustav Vasa's friendly family atmosphere has everything to do with Polish manager Krystyna Öhrling and her Swedish husband, Aarne, and their staff. Rooms have some attractive personal touches, such as an antique radio or a classic free-standing wardrobe. No. 1 is a particularly nice double with bath; no. 3, a comfortable single with the bath just across the hall. Most rooms have safes. At night a video movie is usually shown in the living room. Two blocks from the T-Bana station, wedged between Odengatan and Karlbergsvägen, the hotel is across from the monumental domed Gustav Vasa Church.

3. DOUBLES FOR LESS THAN 500 KR ($90.90)

NORRMALM

HOTELL DANIELSON, Wallingatan 31, S-11124 Stockholm. Tel. 08/11-10-76 or 11-10-65. 14 rms (some with toilet and shower). TEL **Bus:** 47 or 53 from Central Station to 3rd stop.

$ **Rates:** 300 Kr ($54.55) single without toilet or shower, 350 Kr ($63.65) single with toilet but no shower, 400 Kr ($72.70) single with toilet and shower; 400 Kr ($72.70) double without toilet or shower, 500 Kr ($90.90) double with toilet but no shower, 510 Kr ($92.70) double with toilet and shower; 510 Kr ($92.70) triple without toilet or shower, 690 Kr ($125.45) triple with toilet and shower. Breakfast 30 Kr ($5.45) extra. No credit cards.

The Danielson is not in top form: The toilets are small and aging, and the room lighting is dim. Most rooms have a telephone, however, and the location can't be beat—at the corner of Västmannagatan, a few blocks from some of Norrmalm's main shopping streets and 8 blocks (a 10-minute walk) north of Central Station.

WASA PARK HOTEL, Sankt Eriksplan 1, S-11320 Stockholm. Tel. 08/34-02-85. 14 rms (none with bath). TEL TV **T-Bana:** St. Eriksplan, 4 stops from Central Station.

$ **Rates:** 395 Kr ($71.80) single; 520 ($94.55) double. Extra person 150 Kr ($27.30). Breakfast 30 Kr ($5.45) extra, although in summer sometimes included in room rate. EU, MC, V.

The new double rooms here resemble those you might find in a first-class hotel, with sharp gray carpets, dark-wood furniture, and TVs. A few more old-fashioned rooms still remain. All have telephones, and most have TVs. Still, quality varies. The public bathrooms, one with a tub, are quite clean. The carefree manner in which the place is run was slightly disconcerting, but the service was good enough. When business is slow, the management is open to price negotiation. The location, in Norrmalm's arty quarter, is pleasant. You'll find the entrance on Sankt Eriksplan through the arch to the right of the Thai restaurant. The airport bus stops outside, and the T-Bana is a block away.

PENSIONAT ODEN, Odengatan 38, S-11351 Stockholm. Tel. 08/61-24-349. 9 rms (none with bath). **T-Bana:** Odenplan; then walk 4 blocks away from church along Odengatan. **$ Rates:** 375 Kr ($68.20) single; 495 Kr ($90) double. No credit cards.

One of Stockholm's better values, the Oden features large rooms with white-wood furniture in bright, cheery surroundings. The rooms facing the street are nicer but noisier than the ones in the rear. You're likely to feel at home in either. One of the doubles has a refrigerator, and several rooms come with clock radios; no. 7 is an especially comfortable twin. The hotel is on the other end of Odengatan from Wasa Park.

4. ROOMS IN PRIVATE HOMES

Staying in a room in a private home has several advantages: It costs less than a hotel; it offers a more intimate environment than a hotel while providing all-important privacy; and it allows you the pleasure of getting to know your Swedish host and to see how the people live day to day.

It's common for Stockholm's city dwellers to supplement their incomes by sharing their homes with travelers. Not surprisingly, the hosts are most often women, often widowed or divorced; they are also well traveled, quite knowledgeable about the world, and particularly enthusiastic about Stockholm.

There is an unofficial network of private-room renters, so even if the home you call is booked solid, the chances are good that the owner will refer you to a friend who does have a room vacancy. Out of courtesy to hosts, let them know your arrival time so they do not spend unnecessary hours waiting for you. (And be understanding

**FROMMER'S SMART TRAVELER:
ACCOMMODATIONS**

TAKE ADVANTAGE OF THE FOLLOWING:

1. Hostels, two of which are in the center of the city.
2. Rooms in private homes, which often come with kitchen privileges.
3. Room-finding services, which often offer discounted hotel rooms.
4. Hotels whose room rates include breakfast.
5. Weekly rates instead of daily rates, if you plan to be in town any length of time.

if they cannot spend as much time socializing with you as you might like once you do arrive). You'll be more than impressed with the sophistication of both the hosts and the lodging they offer you.

The following companies work with private citizens all around Stockholm and can offer comfortable accommodations at budget prices. Ask for a place near a subway or bus stop:

Hotelljänst, Vasagatan 15-17, 4th floor, 11120 Stockholm (tel. 08/10-44-67; fax 08/21-37-16), regularly rents 50 private rooms and charges excellent set rates of 200 Kr ($36.35) single, and 300 Kr ($54.55) double. There is no service fee, but a minimum 2-night stay is required. Private rooms must be reserved 10 days in advance. The office, which has a 24-hour answering machine, is located 2 long blocks from Central Station. It's open Monday through Thursday from 9am to noon and then from 1 to 5pm (to 4pm on Friday).

All-Rum, Wallingatan 34, 11124 Stockholm (tel. 08/21-37-89 or 21-37-90), managed by Hans Olsson, acts as an agent for about 20 private homes and half a dozen small apartments in Stockholm. Room rates are usually 220 Kr ($40) single, and 450 Kr ($81.82) double. Weekly rates for private apartments with TV and bathrooms are 2,500 Kr ($454.55) single, and 3,500 Kr ($636.36) double. You must come to the office in person for an apartment assignment, but call ahead to verify that space is available. All-Rum is located in the bend of Wallingatan, at the corner of Västmannagatan, about 7 blocks north of Central Station. It is open Monday through Wednesday from 10am to 5pm, on Thursday from 10am to 6pm, and on Friday from 10am to 3pm. The office is closed for 1 or 2 weeks in July.

Note: Most Swedish hosts do not take credit cards, so you'll have to pay in cash or in traveler's checks.

FROMMER'S COOL FOR KIDS
ACCOMMODATIONS

AF *Chapman* (see p. 67) Your kids will love the adventure of staying on board an authentic three-masted, fully rigged schooner. Now a Stockholm landmark, this gallant "tall ship" once sailed under British, Norwegian, and Swedish flags before becoming a hostel in 1949.

Langholmen Youth Hostel and Hotel (see p. 68) How many teenagers can say they've spent the night in jail and not mean their parents' house? This hostel was once a prison that housed Sweden's notoriously wicked criminals. The decor is now an exciting mix of prison institutional and high-tech Scandinavian design. The staff even dresses like inmates.

Touristgården Zinken (see p. 68) The seven bungalows that make up this hostel are situated on grounds with trees, roses, and picnic tables—great for rambunctious kids to play off a little energy. Nearby they'll find a playground, park, bakery, and beach.

Ms. Eivon Lichtshiner (see p. 65) One of her rooms comes with a loftbed for the kids and a convenient kitchenette.

Ms. Erja-Rütta Salonen (see p. 65) If you're staying a week, you can rent a whole apartment in this communal building, which houses 18 Stockholm families (there are lots of native kids around).

Ms. Ingrid Ollen (see p. 66) It's like a visit to Grandma's house, since friendly Ms. Ollen *is* a proud grandma. You get kitchen privileges, and there's an open-air pool nearby.

NORRMALM

MS. EVA GISSLAR, Skeppargatan 49B, S-11458 Stockholm. Tel. 08/663-49-57. 2 rms. **T-Bana:** Östermalmstorg. Take Östermalm exit and then walk 3 blocks (about 5 min.) east to apartment, which is next door to flag shop.

$ Rates: 275 Kr ($50) single; 400 Kr ($72.70) double. Breakfast 25 Kr ($4.55) extra.

This place has it all: a central location, elegant facilities, and an engaging, gracious host. The single room is comfortable, and the double room features a large wooden writing table and a pretty queen-size bed. Guests have use of the kitchen. A lawyer by training, Ms. Gisslar is a consultant to a committee that is dedicated to human-rights causes and awards alternative peace prizes. Having a passion for art, Ms. Gisslar is an avid collector. Be sure to call her ahead of time to book a reservation.

MS. ELIZABET VIKLUND, Roslagsgatan 15, S-11355 Stockholm. Tel. 08/15-40-51. 2 rms. **Bus:** 53 from Central Station (it stops across street from her building).

$ Rates: 225 Kr ($40.90) single; 375 Kr ($68.20) double. Breakfast 25 Kr ($4.55) extra.

⭐ A cordial and informative host, Ms. Viklund will point out the best budget cafes and shops in her neighborhood, a short bus/subway ride from the city center. Her home has the feel of a country house, with large windows, lots of wood furniture, touches of lace, a bottle collection, and dried and fresh flowers everywhere. The White Room is reserved for singles; the double room has an adjacent bath with tub. Ms. Viklund, a fine cook whose guests clamor for recipes, lived and studied in New York in the sixties. One block from her house, there is a bus stop where dozens of buses connect with the Odenplan subway stop.

KUNGSHOLMEN

MS. EIVON LICHTSHINER, Bergsgatan 45, S-11228 Stockholm. Tel. 08/746-91-66. 3 rms. (1 with kitchenette). **T-Bana:** Rådhuset, 1 stop from Central Station; then walk less than 2 blocks.

$ Rates: 300 Kr ($54.55) single; 400 Kr ($72.70) double; 400–500 Kr ($72.70–$90.90) for room with kitchenette, depending on number of guests.

The friendly Ms. Lichtshiner is conversant in English, German, French, and Russian. Each of her comfortable rooms has a toilet, sink, and shower; one that is particularly popular with families has a loftbed and a kitchenette. Guests staying in other rooms have use of Ms. Lichtshiner's kitchen. Additionally, she rents a little "paradise house" in the country, 15 miles outside Stockholm.

SÖDERMALM

MS. ERJA-RÜTTA SALONEN, Bastugatan 31, 3rd floor, S-11725 Stockholm. Tel. 08/658-55-89. 2 rms. TV **T-Bana:** Line 14 from Central Station to Mariatorget (3rd stop); building is 5-minute walk from there up steep hill.

$ Rates: 225 Kr ($40.90) single; 350 Kr ($63.65) double.

If you're interested in communal living, a stay here would be educational as well as pleasant. Eighteen families built, live in, and share meals in this modern structure with an oval glass entry. It has a sauna, communal kitchen and dining area, and round tower with a panoramic view of the city. Of the two rooms that Ms. Salonen rents out, the double is somewhat cramped with a king-size bed and desk; the single has a balcony that overlooks courtyards below. Both rooms have TVs, and they share a large bath with a shower. Guests may use the washing machine and sauna (not the kitchen). Ms. Salonen, who is originally from Finland, prefers that you write ahead. An apartment is available for those who plan to stay a week. Ask about group accommodations.

MS. PERNILLA WILTON, Bastugatan 48A, S-11725 Stockholm. Tel. 08/84-14-79. 1 rm. TV **T-Bana:** Mariatorget; then walk 5 blocks north to Bastugatan.

$ Rates: 200 Kr ($36.35) per person, single or double.

Located in the same residential area as Ms. Salonen's communal building, Ms. Wilton's single accommodation is equipped with a TV and a full-size bed. As there's only one room, be sure to call ahead to see if it's available.

OUTSIDE THE CENTER

MS. INGRID OLLEN, Störtloppsvägen 34, S-12661 Stockholm. Tel. 08/646-68-68. 2 rms. **T-Bana:** Västertorp; exit station following arrow toward Störtloppsvägen. Turn left on Störtloppsvägen and walk 2 blocks; when you reach *apotek* (pharmacy), walk behind building to get to entrance.

$ Rates: 175 Kr ($31.80) single; 250 Kr ($45.45) double; 300 Kr ($54.55) triple.

Located a 15-minute T-Bana ride from the center of Stockholm in a pleasant neighborhood that includes a bank, post office, and several stores and cafes, these two double rooms come with cooking privileges. Ms. Ollen is a retired nurse—not to mention world traveler and avid swimmer—who has welcomed people from 30 countries to her home over the years. Guests may use the laundry for 25 Kr ($4.55), and there is an open-air pool nearby.

5. HOSTELS

"OFFICIAL" IYHF HOSTELS

There are four "official" International Youth Hostel Federation (IYHF) hostels in Stockholm, offering well-maintained, clean lodgings at excellent rates. The two on Skeppsholmen probably offer the best-located accommodations in the city. Because of it, they fill up by 8am in summer. All the hostels are similarly priced and offer lower rates to IYHF cardholders. If you are not a hostel member, you must get a Welcome Card; you will pay an extra 29 Kr ($5.30) per night for up to 6 nights, after which you gain member status. *Note:* The Swedish Hostel Federation emphasizes that its hostels are not just for young people, so if hosteling suits your travel style, age is irrelevant.

AF *CHAPMAN*, Västra Brobänken, Skeppsholmen, S-11149 Stockholm. Tel. 08/10-37-15 or 20-57-05. 136 beds (no rooms with baths). **T-Bana:** Kungsträdgården. **Bus:** 65.

$ Rates: 85 Kr ($15.45) per person with the IYHF card, 117 Kr ($21.30) without. Paper sheets 25 Kr ($4.55) extra; towels 10 Kr ($1.80); breakfast 40 Kr ($7.30). No credit cards. **Closed:** Mid-Dec–Apr 1.

The towering, fully rigged masts of this gallant "tall ship" are a Stockholm landmark. The vessel sailed throughout the world under British, Norwegian, and Swedish flags before being established as a hostel in 1949. Today it is permanently moored on Skeppsholmen. The extremely popular hostel turns away as many as 100 people a day in summer (it's closed in winter), so arrive early (or call a day ahead) to reserve a bed. Reception is open from 7am to noon and then from 3 to 10pm. The rooms are closed daily from 10am to 4pm. There is a 1am curfew and a 5-night maximum stay, after which you can move to the STF Vandrarhem across the street.

Sleeping bags are forbidden; you may rent sheets or supply your own. Each room has a locker, but there is no kitchen, laundry, or TV room—you may wash out small items in sinks and watch TV across the street at the STF Vandrarhem. There are only two showers for women. The common area (as well as the cafe on the deck in summer) is conducive to meeting people. You'll get a lot of sightseeing and money-saving tips by browsing through the budget-conscious *Stockholm Guide* compiled by senior deputy warden Catharina Hård af Segerstad.

STF VANDRARHEM, Västra Brobänken, Skeppsholmen, S-11149 Stockholm. Tel. 08/20-25-06. 152 beds (no rooms with bath). **T-Bana:** Kungsträdgården. **Bus** 65.

$ Rates: 85 Kr ($15.45) per person with IYHF card, 117 Kr ($21.30) without. If available, bed in 15-bed room is bargain at 50 Kr ($9.10). Paper sheets 25 Kr ($4.55) extra; towels 10 Kr ($1.80); breakfast 40 Kr ($7.30). No credit cards. **Closed:** Mid-Dec–mid-Jan.

Located just across the street from the AF *Chapman*, this yellow three-story hostel often picks up the ship's overflow in its 14 doubles, 14 triples, and 14 quads, plus a 15-bed room for men and a 6-bed room for women. The doubles, triples, and quads are of good size and have sinks; some feature magnificent views of Old Town. There are lockers, a small shop for snacks and sundries, museum prints in the rooms and hallways, and several common areas with benches and tables for relaxing or watching TV. The dining room serves terrific porridge (try it the Swedish way, with milk and apple butter). If you like privacy, this hostel provides more of it than the *Chapman*. The reception area is open from 7am to noon and then from 3pm to 10pm. Curfew is at 2am.

LÅNGHOLMEN YOUTH HOSTEL AND HOTEL, Långholmen Island (P.O. Box 9116), S-10272 Stockholm. Tel. 08/668-05-10. Fax 08/84-10-96. TV TEL **T-Bana:** Hornstull; then follow directions below.

$ Rates: In hostel, 85 Kr ($15.45) per person with IYHF card, 117 Kr ($21.30) without. Cotton sheets 37 Kr ($6.70) extra; towels 10 Kr ($1.80); breakfast 50 Kr ($9.10) (half price for children under 12). Hotel rates (including breakfast) daily in summer and Sat–Sun year round, 440 Kr ($80) single cell with shower, 640 ($116.35) double cell with shower; Mon–Fri in spring, fall, and winter, 640 Kr ($116.35) single, 840 Kr ($152.70) double. AE, DC, EU, V.

For more than 250 years, Långholmen prison housed some of Sweden's notoriously wicked criminals. Painstaking renovations, true to the integrity of the building, have culminated in one of the fanciest, most unique hostels in the world. The decor is an enjoyable cross between prison institutional and ultramodern Scandinavian. Most rooms have private baths, TVs, and telephones, as well as brand-new high-quality beds that pull down Murphy-style from the walls.

Långholmen is co-run by the city of Stockholm and the Swedish Hostel Federation, and rents similar rooms at both hostel and hotel prices. Sheets and towels are not provided in the hostel half, and you're expected to clean the hostel room when you leave. Guests may use the kitchen and laundry facilities, and borrow an iron or hairdryer. You may even swim in the lake in front of the hotel. On winter weekdays, when the hotel is full, only 26 beds are available at hostel prices. No curfew is imposed.

From the Hornstull T-Bana station, follow Långholmsgatan toward Västerbroplan. Turn left on Hogalidsgatan, and cross the first small bridge onto the island, a 10-minute walk in all. It's easier to get here by car, but if you're walking the circuitous route, enter the Långholmen compound where you see the glass walkway. During summer, there is boat service from Stadhusbron, near Central Station. Call reception for departure times and to see if beds are available.

TOURISTGÅRDEN ZINKEN, Zinkens Väg 20, S-11741 Stockholm. Tel. 08/68-57-86. 400 beds (no rooms with bath). **T-Bana:** Zinkensdamm; then follow directions below.

$ Rates: 85 Kr ($15.45) per person with IYHF card, 117 Kr ($21.30) without. Cotton sheets 36 Kr ($6.55) extra; towels 10 Kr ($1.80); breakfast 40 Kr ($7.30). No credit cards.

Seven bunk-bedded bungalows make up Touristgården Zinken, the largest hostel in Sweden. Rooms are clean, and a kitchen is available free for guests' use. Several terrific facilities, available at extra cost, include a sauna at 10 Kr ($1.80); a large Jacuzzi and solarium at 35 Kr ($6.35); and washing machines at 29 Kr ($5.25). Reception sells snacks and postcards. The ambience is that of a simple country lodge; the staff is friendly; and the grounds are filled with picnic tables, roses, and trees. The hostel is open 24 hours.

From the Zinkensdamm T-Bana station, walk east along Hornsgatan (you might want to make a quick stop at the bakery) following the rock outcropping. Turn left down the steps between nos. 103 and 107, and follow the path down the hill. The hostel is the brown building on the left. It's on western Södermalm; as always, call ahead before setting out.

"UNOFFICIAL" HOSTELS

NORRMALM

BRYGGHUSET, Norrtullsgatan 12N, Stockholm. Tel. 08/ 31-24-24. Fax 08/33-29-74. 57 beds. **T-Bana:** Odenplan; take Odenplan exit and walk 3 blocks up Norrtullsgatan.
$ Rates: 100 Kr ($18.20) per adult, 85 Kr ($15.45) per child. Sheets 25 Kr ($4.55) extra. No credit cards. **Open:** Early June–Aug.

Most of the year, the building serves as a community center where locals gather for various events. During the summer, the community is expanded to include world travelers, who are accommodated in two-, three-, four-, and six-bed rooms. This is a practical place for families, as there are laundry facilities here. The atmosphere and prices are inviting, and breakfast is available next door for 30 Kr ($5.45). It's open from early June to the end of August (call for exact dates), and a 2am curfew is enforced. The entrance is right on the main street, near the corner of Frejgatan.

SÖDERMALM

***GUSTAF* AF *KLINT*, Söder Mälarstrand, S-11630 Stock-holm. Tel. 08/640-40-77** or 640-40-78. Fax 08/640-64-16. 32 cabins (none with bath). **T-Bana:** Slussen; then walk down to riverbank—ship is about 200 yards to right.
$ Rates: In the hostel, 110 Kr ($20) per person. Paper sheets 35 Kr ($6.35) extra; cotton sheets 55 Kr ($10); towels 10 Kr ($3); breakfast 40 Kr ($7.30). In the hotel, 350 ($63.65) single; 480 Kr ($87.30) double. AE, DC, EU, MC, V.

This floating hotel and youth hostel rigged with lights is on the riverbank just across from Old Town. When the *Klint* served as a radar sounder mapping out the ocean floor, the officers lived in what is now the hotel part of the ship (five singles and nine doubles), while the deckhands occupied what now serves as the hostel (two doubles, a triple, and 15 quads). The hotel section is slightly more spacious than the hostel's cramped quarters, and all cabins are equipped with bunk beds. During the summer, the ship's decktop cafe provides a lovely view of Stockholm Harbor. Year round, below deck, cheap dinners are served in a small but smokey restaurant. The location is convenient; and general manager Karl-Olof Olofsson, who lives aboard, is congenial and helpful.

COLUMBUS HOTELL AND VANDRARHEM, Tjärhovsgatan 11, S-11621 Stockholm. Tel. 08/44-17-17. Fax 08/702-07-64. 44 rms (none with bath). **T-Bana:** Medborgarplatsen; the hostel is 5 blocks east on Tjärhovsgatan.

$ Rates: In the hostel, 250 Kr ($45.45) single or double; 105 Kr ($19.10) per person in family or dorm rooms. Paper sheets cost 25 Kr ($4.55) extra; cotton sheets 40 Kr ($7.30); towels 10 Kr ($1.80); breakfast 35 Kr ($5.35). In the hotel, 390 Kr ($70.90) single; 490 Kr ($89.10) double. No credit cards. **Closed:** Dec 22–Jan 1.

Another hotel and hostel in one, the Columbus is capably and cordially run by brothers Dan and Bjorn Collin. The hotel section, in a quiet area separate from the hostel, consists of only four rooms (three doubles and one single) that share a shower and toilet; each has a TV but no phone. The hostel features rooms with one to six beds and lockers. There are three showers for men and women on each of the hostel's three floors; the public bathrooms are passable but not sparkling. Amenities include a secure baggage room, a small kitchen for guests that is open 24 hours, and a room with a sun bed for those desirous of an artificial Nordic tan. You'll also find a pleasant cafe for meals or snacks, an outdoor cafe in summer, a children's playground, and a nearby park and indoor pool.

---

6. WEEKEND & SUMMER DISCOUNTS

During the summer months and year round on weekends, when there's less business travel, the hotels listed in this section reduce their rates—making them a good value for the budget traveler. Otherwise, they are outside our $50-a-day budget.

NORRMALM

QUEEN'S HOTEL, Drottninggatan 71A, S-11136 Stockholm. Tel. 08/24-94-60. Fax 08/21-76-20. 20 rms (11 with toilet and shower). TV TEL **Directions:** 10-minute walk from

Central Station; turn left on Vasagatan, right on Olof Palmes Gata, and left again on Drottninggatan.

$ Rates (including breakfast): Every day in summer and Sat–Sun year round, 400 Kr ($72.70) single without bath, 500 Kr ($90.90) single with toilet and shower; 500 Kr ($90.90) double without bath, 600 Kr ($109.10) double with toilet and shower. Mon–Fri in spring, fall, and winter, prices rise about 15%. ACCESS, DC, EU, MC, V.

You can't get more central than this location—at the intersection of Stockholm's busiest shopping street and Olof Palmes Gata. This pleasant, but not fancy, hotel has 16 double and 4 small single rooms, a TV lounge, and an old-fashioned elevator. Rooms are well furnished, and no. 20 is particularly inviting. Breakfast is served in a cheerful country-style dining room. Manager Camilla Stenemyr heads up a friendly English-speaking staff.

SÖDERMALM

HOTELL ANNO 1647, Mariagrånd 3, S-11646 Stockholm. Tel. 08/44-04-80. Fax 08/43-37-00. Telex 12550. 43 rms (21 with bath). TV TEL **T-Bana:** Slussen.

$ Rates (including breakfast): Every day in summer and Fri–Sat year round, 420 Kr ($76.35) single without bath, 520 Kr ($94.55) single with bath; 520 Kr ($94.55) double without bath, 680 Kr ($123.65) double with bath. Sun–Thurs in spring, fall, and winter, prices double. AE, DC, EU, MC, V.

This gorgeous old hotel has undergone many renovations since 1647. And while updating has made it more modern and expensive, the Anno still protectively guards its country-inn roots. The rooms with private bath are much nicer than those without. Still, all rooms are more than adequate, with pretty hardwood floors, tasteful furnishings in mauve and green or gray, TVs, telephones, radios, desks, and good reading lights. There is a nonsmoking floor. One hitch: no elevator. If you dislike climbing stairs, ask for a double room on the ground floor. Many of the rooms have sweeping views of the harbor and Old Town. The entrance is in the rear, on narrow Mariagrånd.

7. LONG-TERM STAYS

The apartment situation in Stockholm is horrendous and it's tough to find a place, whether your goal is short- or long-term. Your best bet is to contact an agency that deals in short-term rentals, and then see how long you can stretch out your stay.

All-Rum, Wallingatan 34, 11124 Stockholm (tel. 08/21-37-89 or 21-37-90), managed by Hans Olsson, acts as an agent for about half a dozen small apartments in Stockholm. Weekly rates for private flats with TVs and bathrooms are 2,500 Kr ($454.55) single and 3,500 Kr ($636.36) double. You must come to the office in person for an apartment assignment, but call ahead to verify that space is available. All-Rum is located in the bend of Wallingatan, at the corner of Västmannagatan, about 7 blocks north of Central Station. It is open Monday through Wednesday from 10am to 5pm, on Thursday from 10am to 6pm, and on Friday from 10am to 3pm. The office is closed for 1 or 2 weeks in July.

Also contact **Hotelljänst,** Vasagatan 15-17 (tel. 10-44-67), or **Bo-Tjänst,** Kungstensgatan 40 (tel. 3-25-05).

8. WORTH THE EXTRA BUCKS

NORRMALM

ÖSTERMALMS PENSIONAT, Sibyllegatan 19. S-11442 Stockholm. Tel. 08/660-30-89. 7 rms (none with bath). TV **T-Bana:** Östermalmstorg.

$ Rates (including breakfast): 425 Kr ($77.20) single; 595 Kr ($108.20) double. Extra person 50 Kr ($9.10) in family room (sleeps 5). No credit cards.

Östermalms Pensionat offers old-style rooms with large windows, quilted beds, blond-wood floors, and touches that might include an antique couch, old wooden furniture, or even a ceramic stove. Besides the lovely ambience, the public bathrooms (one with a tub) are immaculately clean. There are food lockers in the kitchen, and refrigerators and TVs in the rooms (two also have sinks). Guests can enjoy the TV/breakfast room, and they have complimentary use of the washing machine. Because of its great location and attractive rooms, Östermalms Pensionat is highly recommended, but its small size makes calling ahead for reservations a must. It's on the third floor of a yellow building across from a beautiful domed church called Hedvig Eleonara. Room no. 3 looks out on the church; no. 1 is particularly quiet.

WELLINGTON HOTEL, Storgatan 6, 114 51 Stockholm. Tel. 08/667-09-10. Fax 08/667-12-54. Telex 10145. 51 rooms (all with bath with shower; a few with tub) TEL TV **T-Bana:** Östermalmstorg.

$ Rates (including breakfast): May through September, with Best Western Hotel Cheque, $60.45 per person. Otherwise, 1,100 Kr ($200) single; 1,400 Kr ($254.55) double. AE, MC, V.

Except for the economical Hotel Cheques offered by Best Western, the prices charged at this small hotel would far exceed budget status. The staff is so friendly that guests often linger in the living room–like lobby. From the comfortable rooms—in muted colors (gray, mauve, purple, blue, salmon, tan) and outfitted with a pants press and hairdryer—you can hear the soft sound of church bells on the hour. A sauna, free to guests, is beautifully appointed with an outer changing room, terrycloth robes, plush towels, lotion and shampoo, shower, toilet, and sun bed. Also available: concierge service, an ironing room, two nonsmoking floors, and the most pleasant electronic wake-up call you're ever likely to get. The top floors provide memorable rooftop views.

STOCKHOLM DINING

Food in Stockholm is priced higher than in most other European cities, so visitors on a budget have to choose with care. This hardly means you'll starve, though, because in addition to good-value lunch specials, there are a number of dependable budget eateries.

With price limitations, you may not be able to enjoy a full-fledged Swedish smorgasbord, but you can look forward to trying a number of other local specialties including herring (*strömming*), pea soup (called *ärtsoppa,* and usually served on Thursday), eel, Swedish meatballs, dill meat fricassee, and simple, tasty meat-and-potato hash (*pytt i panna*).

If you're in Stockholm during the Christmas season, be sure to sample ginger cookies and *glögg,* a potent traditional drink of fortified hot mulled wine with raisins and almonds. And year round, make it a point to visit the Swedish pastry shops—some of the best in Europe.

Many restaurants compete for noontime midweek business with fantastic lunch specials. Most cost 45 to 60 Kr ($8.20 to $10.90), and that usually includes a main course, salad, bread, and a nonalcoholic drink. If you don't see a daily special (*dagens rätt*) posted, ask for it.

At most of the places listed below, reservations are not necessary—or even accepted. Taxes and tip are included in the price on the menu. Restaurants are usually open for lunch from 11am to 2pm and for dinner from 6 to 11pm; vegetarian restaurants close earlier (check individual listings). For maximum savings at mealtime, avoid alcohol; state control in Sweden keeps prices astronomically high.

1. MEALS FOR LESS THAN 50 KR [$9.10]

NORRMALM AND ÖSTERMALM

NIKKI'S CAFE, Jungfrugatan 6. Tel. 662-14-74.
  Cuisine: LIGHT FARE. **T-Bana:** Östermalmstorg.
$ **Prices:** Breakfast 14–28 Kr ($2.55–$5.10); sandwiches 14–21 Kr ($2.55–$3.80); hefty salad 40 Kr ($7.30); daily special 47 Kr ($8.55).
  Open: Mon–Fri 7:30am–2:30pm. **Closed:** 5 weeks in summer, usually July to early Aug.

The hours aren't great, but the prices are. This tiny cafe, tucked just off the main drag and half a block from Hedvig Eleonara Church, has only nine tables, red-and-white-checked table cloths, and red hanging lamps. Prices are reasonable (for Stockholm), especially if you like breakfast; coffee and tea are 6 Kr ($1.10) for the first cup, 4 Kr (70¢) for a refill. The special comes with bread and coffee. Help yourself to the veggies on the table.

SILVERHÄSTEN CAFE, Mäster Samuelsgatan 21. Tel. 20-23-74.
  Cuisine: LIGHT FARE. **T-Bana:** T-Centralen.
$ **Prices:** 36–51 Kr ($6.55–$9.30). EU, MC.
  Open: Mon–Thurs 8am–11pm, Fri–Sat 9am–5am, Sun 11am–11pm.
From outside it appears to be a small cafe, but inside it consists of five different eating areas, each of which attracts a different crowd—readers, chatterers, diners, a young group, an older group. Fare includes crepes, sandwiches in croissants, lasagne, pasta, stuffed potatoes, large salads, milkshakes, and fresh-squeezed juices. Order at the counter and bus your own table. There's piano music at Saturday lunch.

COFFEE HOUSE, Odengatan 45 (near Dobelnsgatan). Tel. 32-53-43.
  Cuisine: LIGHT FARE. **T-Bana:** Odenplan.
$ **Prices:** 32–45 Kr ($5.80–$8.80); lunch special 32 Kr ($5.80).
  Open: Mon–Fri 7am–7pm, Sat 9am–5pm, Sun 10am–4pm.
This friendly place, with tiled floor and round tables, is filled with local folks and the low hum of conversation. The lunch special, served from 11am to 2pm, includes a sandwich, juice, and coffee. Quiche and large salads are also available, and coffee comes with a free refill (help yourself from the table near the door). There's a high

To Drott-
← ningholm

← To Lake
Mälar

SWEDEN	Alice B.	Cafe Pan	Hard Rock Café
	Arnolds	Capri	Hötorgs Hallen
Stockholm	Bakfickan	City Lejon	Kungshallen
	Bombay Kebab	Coffee House	Kungstornet
	Cafe Blå Porten	Grona Linjen	Le Bistrot de Wasahof

chair for tots. The Lebanese owners, the three Makdessi-Elias
brothers, will make you feel most welcome.

KUNGSTORNET, Kungsgatan 28. Tel. 20-66-43.

Cuisine: LIGHT FARE. **T-Bana:** Hötorget.

$ Prices: 18–47 Kr ($3.30–$8.55). Daily special, 44 Kr ($8).

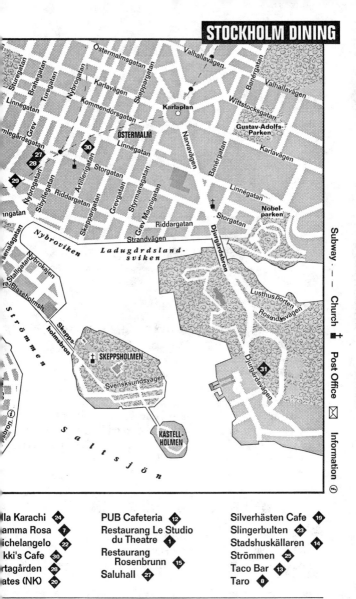

lla Karachi 🔶24
amma Rosa 🔶7
ichelangelo 🔶22
kki's Cafe 🔶30
rtagården 🔶26
ates (NK) 🔶20

PUB Cafeteria 🔶12
Restaurang Le Studio du Theatre 🔶1
Restaurang Rosenbrunn 🔶15
Saluhall 🔶27

Silverhästen Cafe 🔶19
Slingerbulten 🔶23
Stadshuskällaren 🔶14
Strömmen 🔶25
Taco Bar 🔶13
Taro 🔶8

Open: Mon–Thurs 7am–11pm, Fri 7am–midnight, Sat 8am–midnight, Sun 9am–10pm.

What you see is what you get: a blue neon sign out front, décor from the fifties, seating upstairs and down, and a menu heavy on sandwiches. You can also get quiche and salads, and the special comes with salad, bread, and coffee. It's a block from Sveavätan.

SÖDERMALM

BOMBAY KEBAB, Varvsgatan 3. Tel. 658-62-80.
  Cuisine: INDIAN. **T-Bana:** Hornstull.
$ Prices: 25–55 Kr ($4.55–$10); lunch special 35 Kr ($6.35).
  Open: Mon–Sat 11am–midnight, Sun 1pm–midnight.

Ⓢ This place can't be beat on several counts: The food's good, plentiful, and includes favorites like shish kebab, beef vindaloo, biriani, samosa, and vegetarian dishes; the price is right; and it's open late.

---

2. MEALS FOR LESS THAN 70 KR [$12.70]

GAMLA STAN

LILLA KARACHI, Lilla Nygatan 12. Tel. 20-54-54.
  Cuisine: PAKISTANI. **T-Bana:** Gamla Stan.
$ Prices: 45–70 Kr ($8.20–$12.70).
  Open: Mon–Fri 11am–7pm, Sat–Sun noon–7pm.

★ This small, well-decorated restaurant with top-notch Swedish-influenced Pakistani cuisine is one of Stockholm's greatest bargains. The aroma alone will start you salivating even before you sit down at one of the cozy glass-topped tables. Lilla Karachi is especially recommended for its lunch prices and vegetarian meals. The restaurant is near the corner of Tyska Brinken, about 2 blocks from the T-Bana station.

NORRMALM & ÖSTERMALM

CITY LEJON, Holländargatan 8. Tel. 20-76-35.
  Cuisine: SWEDISH. **T-Bana:** Hötorget.
$ Prices: 44–70 Kr ($8–$12.70); lunch specials from 39 Kr ($7.10).
  Open: Mon–Thurs 10am–10pm, Fri 10am–11pm, Sat noon–11pm, Sun noon–10pm.

The great draw here is the lunch special, absolutely one of the best values in town. This place bustles, mainly with local office workers, and gets quite busy around noon. A continuous series of wooden doors covers the restaurant's walls, complemented by wooden tables and low-wattage hanging lamps of Middle Eastern design. The food is good and filling—the wienerschnitzel and plank steak are particularly popular—and the location is great, just off Kungsgatan, 3 blocks north of Hötorget Square.

CAPRI, Nybrogatan 15. Tel. 662-31-32.

Cuisine: ITALIAN. **Reservations:** Suggested at night. **T-Bana:** Östermalmstorg.

$ Prices: 60–70 Kr ($10.90–$12.70); pizza or pasta lunch special (including small glass of milk or beer, salad, bread, and coffee) 55 Kr ($10). AE, DC, EU, MC, V.

Open: Mon–Fri 11am–midnight, Sat–Sun noon–midnight; lunch special 11am–3pm (unless food gives out earlier).

Although this place also serves meat and fish dishes, it's the extensive pasta and pizza menu—not to mention courteous service and well-prepared dishes—that attracts budgeteers. If you come for dinner, look for the nightly special, which is usually less expensive than the regular menu. With a vaulted ceiling vaguely reminiscent of Italy's Blue Grotto, the restaurant is located just west of the Östermalm food hall (Saluhall) and is 2 blocks from the Östermalmstorg T-Bana station.

GRÖNA LINJEN, Mäster Samuelsgatan 10. Tel. 11-27-90.

Cuisine: VEGETARIAN. **T-Bana:** Östermalmstorg.

$ Prices: All-you-can-eat meal (including main dish, soup, and salad bar)—lunch 60 Kr ($10.90), dinner 70 Kr ($12.70).

Open: Mon–Fri 10:30am–8pm, Sat 11am–8pm.

This was the house of Sweden's prewar Conservative party leader, and you still feel as if you're dining in a private home. The restaurant, which opened as Sweden's first vegetarian establishment in 1940, features vintage ceramic fixtures; white furniture; pastel walls; four dining areas, including a reading room (don't miss the fireplace in the middle room); and an unlimited and varied supply of delicious foods. Enter through a modest doorway near the corner of Norrlandsgatan. The restaurant is on the second floor.

MAMMA ROSA, Sveavägen 55. Tel. 30-40-21.

Cuisine: ITALIAN. **Reservations:** Suggested at night. **T-Bana:** Rådmansgatan.

$ Prices: Pizza and pasta 53–75 Kr ($11.95–$13.65); fish and meat dishes 110–170 Kr ($20–$30.90); lunch special (including bread, salad, espresso, and small glass of beer, juice, or soda) 49–79 Kr ($8.90–$13.35).

Open: Mon–Fri 10:30am–midnight, Sat–Sun noon–midnight; lunch special 10:30am–2:30pm.

A refurbished Stockholm standard, it features gray-and-peach decor, sconces, mirrored walls, and a gleaming cappuccino machine. An authentic Italian staff, a good menu, and great food are the real testaments to this trattoria's success. An attractive special packs 'em in at lunchtime, but to stay under budget at dinner, limit yourself to pasta and pizza. The restaurant is half a block from the Rådmansgatan T-Bana station.

SÖDERMALM

STRÖMMEN, Södermalms Torg. Tel. 43-44-70.
   Cuisine: SWEDISH. **T-Bana:** Slussen.
$ Prices: 39–60 Kr ($7.10–$10.90); lunch special 45 Kr ($8.20).
   Open: Mon–Fri 7:30am–6:30pm, Sat 7:30am–5pm, Sun 9am–6pm.

⑤ It's a coffee shop with a rooftop-restaurant view, and its perch above the harbor—in the free-standing blue building across the square from the Slussen T-Bana station—is one of the best locations in Stockholm. In addition to some of the cheapest dinner main courses in town, Strömmen serves a good breakfast. If you're in the mood for an early-morning walk across Gamla Stan, make this your goal for coffee and a roll. Lunch comes with beer or mineral water, and every seat has a panoramic view.

CAFE PAN, Götgatan 11. Tel. 40-10-32.
   Cuisine: VEGETARIAN. **T-Bana:** Slussen; turn left as you exit station, and left again on Götgatan, a total of 3 blocks. Look for entrance in middle of block.
$ Prices: Soup and bread 45 Kr ($8.20); all-you-can-eat salad bar 55 Kr ($10); all-you-can-eat dinner buffet 70 Kr ($14.20).
   Open: Mon–Sat 11am–9pm, Sun 1–9pm.

Thankfully, this special restaurant is off the main tourist track: Its authentic, cultured atmosphere could never survive the hordes that would descend daily for great food at even better prices. Pan is a vegetarian restaurant and meeting place for the liberal-minded where the all-you-can-eat dinner buffet is hard to beat. The atmosphere is comfortable, and there is dining upstairs and down.

DJURGÅRDEN

CAFE BLÅ PORTEN, Djurgårsvägen 64. Tel. 662-71-62.
   Cuisine: SWEDISH. **Bus:** 44.
$ Prices: 40–70 Kr ($7.30–$12.70).
   Open: Tues and Thurs 11am–9pm, Wed and Fri 11am–4:30pm (until 9pm on Wed in summer), Sat–Sun 11am–5pm.

There are not many restaurants on this museum island, and the ones that are here cater almost exclusively to hungry, stranded tourists.

With this in mind, the cafeteria-style Cafe Blå Porten is the area's best "budget" eatery, serving soup, salads, quiche, and cold meals. It is located in front of the Liljevalch Art Gallery.

IN THE DEPARTMENT STORES

Department-store cafes in Stockholm are a far cry from the Woolworth counters back home. Most are quiet and well decorated, and some are even moderately priced. Here are two in-store suggestions.

PLATES, on 4th floor of NK department store, at Hamngatan 18–20. Tel. 762-80-00.
   Cuisine: LIGHT FARE. **T-Bana:** Kungsträdgården.
$ Prices: 36–85 Kr ($6.55–$15.45).
   Open: Mon–Fri 11am–5pm, Sat–Sun 11am–4pm; lunch special 11am–3pm.
Cheerful, relaxed, and brightly lit, it offers salads, seafood, turkey, Greek dishes, cottage-cheese plates, soup, and sandwiches, as well as a daily soup-and-sandwich special. Sandwiches (and lower prices) are also available at the cafeteria adjacent to Plates and in the coffee shop in the subbasement, which is particularly popular with students.

PUB CAFETERIA, 5th floor of PUB department store, Drottninggatan 72–76, Hörtoget Square. Tel. 791-60-00.
   Cuisine: LIGHT FARE. **T-Bana:** Hötorget.
$ Prices: Daily special 53 Kr ($9.65); other dishes 50–60 Kr ($9.10–$10.90).
   Open: Mon–Fri 10am–7pm, Sat 10am–5pm, Sun 10am–4pm.
A pleasant cafeteria—right beside an exhibit on Greta Garbo, the store's most famous salesperson—it has daily lunch specials and, even better, free coffee refills. PUB fills two buildings; you want the one called Hötogshuset.

EXTRA-SPECIAL LUNCH SPECIALS

Stockholm's ubiquitous lunch specials are its saving grace for the budget traveler. Except for those in most heavily touristed areas, almost every restaurant in the city offers a good lunch at prices that are substantially lower than dinner tariffs. Three of the four restaurants listed below, like most of the city's best deals, are in the business district of eastern Norrmalm. When striking out on your own, note that a crowded restaurant usually means good meals at low prices. The following eateries are above our budget at dinnertime but offer excellent lunch specials.

ALICE B., Sveavägen 57. Tel. 31-55-33.

Cuisine: CONTINENTAL. **Reservations:** Recommended at night. **T-Bana:** Rådmansgatan. **Bus:** 52.

$ Prices: Lunch special 45 Kr ($8.20). AE, DC, EU, MC, V.

Open: Lunch Mon–Fri 11am–3pm; dinner Mon–Tues and Thurs 6pm–midnight, Wed and Fri–Sat 6pm–1am.

Well-prepared, creative lunches are served in this outstanding restaurant housed in Stockholm's gay center. The menu changes daily, so emphasis is on freshness, and all lunches include bread, salad, fruit, and a nonalcoholic drink. See "Networks & Resources" in Chapter 3 for more details. The gay center is half a block from the Rådmansgatan T-Bana station on a pretty tree-lined street. Look for the sign that says "Pride."

RESTAURANG ROSENBRUNN, Brunnsgatan 21. Tel. 11-16-37.

Cuisine: SWEDISH. **T-Bana:** Hötorget.

$ Prices: Lunch special 48 Kr ($8.70). AE, EU, MC, V.

Open: Mon 10:30am–3pm, Tues–Sat 10:30am–11pm; lunch special served Mon–Fri 10:30am–1pm.

À la carte dishes cost 70 to 125 Kr ($12.70 to $22.70) at dinner, but at lunchtime they are served with bread, salad, and a nonalcoholic drink for a half to a third the price. Needless to say, this smart serve-yourself place gets crowded. Rosenbrunn is at the corner of Regeringsgatan, 4 blocks east of Hötorget Square.

BAKFICKAN, Operahuset, Kungsträdgården. Tel. 20-77-45.

Cuisine: SWEDISH.

$ Prices: Specials, served all day, 49–82 Kr ($8.90–$14.90). AE, DC, EU, MC, V.

Open: Mon–Sat 11:30am–11:30pm.

This "Back Pocket" bar and restaurant is little more than an afterthought to the bustling Opera Cafe in the same building.

A popular lunch spot with Stockholm's business folk, it seats only about 20 people, gets crowded quickly, and seems to stay that way. The slowest, quietest time here is from 2 to 5pm, so schedule a late lunch if you can. Otherwise, try to sit at the bar, where service is faster. Specials include venison and salmon with vegetables and bread. The menu is posted in Swedish but make it easier on yourself and ask for the one printed in both Swedish and English. The special is served all day long.

TARO, Kammakargatan 11. Tel. 11-05-15.

Cuisine: JAPANESE. **T-Bana:** Rådmansgatan. **Bus:** 52.

$ Prices: Lunch special 50–55 Kr ($9.10–$10).

Open: Lunch Mon–Fri 11am–1pm; dinner Mon–Sat 4–10pm.
Closed: Fri lunch in winter.

A good lunch spot in the middle of Norrmalm for those with a yen for Japanese food. A choice of three specials served in traditional surroundings includes main course, salad, rice, and green tea. The relaxed atmosphere here is atypical of Stockholm's usual midday rush. The restaurant is just off Sveavägen, 2½ blocks from the Rådmansgatan T-Bana station.

3. MEALS FOR LESS THAN 100 KR ($18.20)

GAMLA STAN

SLINGERBULTEN, Stora Nygatan 24. Tel. 10-76-22.
Cuisine: SWEDISH. **Reservations:** Suggested at dinner. **T-Bana:** Gamla Stan.
$ Prices: 59–160 Kr ($10.70–$29.10); lunch special 45–58 Kr ($8.20–$10.55). AE, DC, EU, MC, V.
Open: Daily 11am–11pm; lunch special 11am–3pm.

 Slingerbulten offers excellent food at moderate prices right in the heart of Old Town. Two small green rooms decorated with plants, paintings depicting Old Town scenes, and checked tablecloths give this place a homey, local flavor. Lunch specials change daily, but the emphasis is on seafood; you always serve yourself at lunch. Dinner is more formal and more expensive, with main courses that include fried herring, Indian-style shrimp with curry and cognac, and trout that is fried and then poached in wine. Stora Nygatan is Gamla Stan's widest street, on the west side of the tiny island. The restaurant (ask them what the name means) is 3 blocks from the Gamla Stan T-Bana station.

FROMMER'S SMART TRAVELER: RESTAURANTS

1. Lunch specials, a long-standing Stockholm tradition, include several filling courses and are considerably less expensive than dinner.
2. Department store cafeterias, pasta-and-pizza houses, and vegetarian restaurants are budget best bets for dinner.

MICHELANGELO, Västerlånggatan 62. Tel. 21-50-99.
   Cuisine: ITALIAN. **T-Bana:** Gamla Stan.
   $ Prices: Pizza and pastas 65–80 Kr ($11.80–$14.55); meat and
   fish dishes 116–179 Kr ($21.10–$32.55); lunch special 50 Kr
   ($9.10). AE, DC, EU, MC, V.
   Open: Mon–Fri 11am–midnight, Sat–Sun and holidays noon–
   midnight; lunch special Mon–Fri 11am–2:30pm.

Stucco walls, pictures of the Sistine Chapel, Italian rock and roll, and
candle-lit tables are the hallmarks of this touristy but good Italian
restaurant. Downstairs, you can eat in one of several brick cellar
rooms with fish tanks and cherub statuettes. The food includes a
large assortment of pizza, pasta with smoked salmon and lobster
sauce, and steak with cream sauce and onions. It's located on the
main pedestrian drag, right in the heart of Old Town and a 2-minute
walk from the Gamla Stan T-Bana station.

NORRMALM & ÖSTERMALM

ARNOLD'S, Birger Jarlsgatan 20. Tel. 24-01-00.
   Cuisine: CONTINENTAL. **T-Bana:** Östermalmstorg.
   $ Prices: 35–95 Kr ($6.35–$17.30). AE, DC, EU, MC, V.
   Open: Mon–Sat 11am–1am.

In this inviting corner restaurant, which is especially crowded in the
evening, the dining area is surrounded by windows looking out onto
lively Stureplan. Childhood memorabilia adorn the walls and ceiling,
and there is additional seating in the upstairs balcony. The stuffed
baked potatoes at lunch are filling, and the price of beer, at 30 Kr
($5.45) for half a liter, is notable. The steaks here, the heftiest item
price-wise, are also popular.

**RESTAURANG LE STUDIO DU THEATRE, Sankt Eriksplan
   4. Tel. 33-63-05.**
   Cuisine: SWEDISH. **Reservations:** Recommended Sat–Sun.
   T-Bana: St. Eriksplan.
   $ Prices: 60–95 Kr ($10.90–$17.30); lunch special 52 Kr ($9.45).
   AE, DC, EU, MC, V.
   Open: Mon–Fri 11am–1am, Sat noon–1am, Sun 2pm–1am;
   lunch special 11am–3pm.

Le Studio is an appealing local place popular with theater-goers (there
are numerous stages in the area). Warm and lively, the room seems
full even when business is slow—which is rare. The restaurant's
intimate size gives it an air of exclusivity, and smart decor complements the good cooking. The wine list is extensive, and at night an
American or Irish bartender can mix your favorite drink. During
summer, café tables line the street and the crowd flows out the door.
Beware a cup of tea here will run you 20 Kr ($3.65). The restaurant is
located by St. Eriksplan square, a few doors from the St. Eriksplan
T-Bana station.

HARD ROCK CAFE, Sveavägen 75. Tel. 16-03-15.

Cuisine: AMERICAN. **T-Bana:** Rådmansgatan.
$ Prices: 79–119 Kr ($14.35–$21.65).
Open: Sun–Mon 11am–midnight, Tues–Sat 11am–2am, Sun 11am–1am.

Is it a tourist attraction or a restaurant? Cynics hate to admit it, but the Hard Rock is perennially packed and, price aside, flips the best burgers in town. The cafe does have character, and whether you like it or not, the chain has successfully promoted itself as the unofficial American embassy to the culinary world. It's located at the corner of Odengatan, 2 blocks north of the Rådmansgatan T-Bana station.

ÖRTAGÅRDEN [Herb Garden], Nybrogatan 31. Tel. 662-17-28.

Cuisine: VEGETARIAN. **Reservations:** Recommended at night. **T-Bana:** Östermalmstorg.
$ Prices: All-you-can-eat mini-smorgasbord 60 Kr ($10.90) Mon–Fri until 5pm, 80 Kr ($14.55) Mon–Fri after 5pm and all day Sat and Sun. DC, EU, MC, V.
Open: Mon–Fri 10:30am–11:30pm, Sat 11am–8:30pm, Sun noon–8:30pm.

Floral furniture, pastel-green woodwork, and a ceiling hung with glass chandeliers may convince you that you're out of your price bracket. Wrong. Örtagården offers one of the best deals in town with its huge all-you-can-eat smorgasbord and comfortable surroundings. Help yourself to the hot and cold foods and take a seat in the elegant dining room. A classical pianist performs at night—reservations are suggested. Örtagården is on the second floor of the same building as the Östermalm food hall (Saluhall), but it has a separate entrance.

4. SPECIALTY DINING

LOCAL BUDGET BETS/FAVORITE MEALS

Bombay Kebab, Varvsgatan 3 (tel. 658-62-80), is tops among youth hostelers for price and quantity. Office workers pack into **City Lejon,** Holländargatan 8 (tel. 20-76-35), for its hearty, economical lunches. Tops among the Italian restaurants in Stockholm are **Capri,** Nybrogatan 15 (tel. 62-31-32), which invites lingering, and **Mamma Rosa,** Sveavägen 55 (tel. 30-40-21); both have stellar service. The **PUB Cafeteria,** in the PUB department store, Drottninggatan 72-76 (tel. 791-60-00), gets raves for the free coffee refills. **Coffee House,** Odengatan 45 (tel. 32-53-43), gives one free coffee refill, too. In Gamla Stan (Old Town), **Slingerbulten,** Stora Nygatan 24 (tel.

10-76-22), is tops for its easygoing, homespun atmosphere. The city's **vegetarian restaurants** (see individual listings) are equally appealing: pretty and not pricey.

FAST-FOOD CHOICES

High-quality fast-food eateries are clustered around Hötorget Square. On the south side of the square, there is **Hötorgs Hallen;** enter through the glass doors and take the escalator down, descending into a cornucopia of prepared foreign foods. Try a kebab in pita or a falafel, a filo-dough pastry, or a Turkish burger, filled with falafel balls, Turkish meats, or lamb. **Piccolino Cafe,** by the escalator, sells sandwiches and a daily hot meal. Hötorgs Hallen is open Monday through Thursday from 9:30am to 6pm, and on Friday and Saturday from 9am to 3pm (during summer, on Saturday until 2pm).

Across Hötorget Square is **Kungshallen,** a two-story indoor mall packed with low-cost fast-food stands selling chicken salad, stuffed crepes, pizzas, pastas, and more. It's open Monday through Friday from 10:30am to 7pm, and on Saturday and Sunday from 11am to 7pm (a couple of stalls stay open until 4am nightly).

Taco Bar, Slöjdgatan 2 (tel. 11-16-26), near Hötorget Square, serves nachos, enchiladas, tacos, and the like in a surprisingly inviting atmosphere. You're a long way from Old Mexico so don't expect *platos excelentes*. Take the T-Bana to Hötorget and walk to Taco Bar; Slöjdgatan is a small street parallel to Sergelgatan. There are smaller versions at Kungsgatan 3 (at Birger Jarlsgatan) and at Kungsgatan 44.

SELF-SERVICE CAFETERIAS

The **NK** and **PUB** department stores both have self-service cafeterias that are tucked off the main drag and are smaller and more intimate than most other cafeterias; see individual listings under "In the Department Stores" in Section 2 of this chapter.

DINING COMPLEX

The **Saluhall,** in a striking brick building at the corner of Nybrogatan and Humlegårdsgatan, is filled with almost two dozen stalls, many doubling as restaurant/cafes. This is the fanciest food market in Stockholm, not to mention the oldest in Sweden (drop by to admire the building if nothing else), and you can rest assured the food here is as fresh as the ambience is unique. Sample *flaskpannkaka* (oven pancake with ham), *frestelse* (baked anchovies and potatoes in cream), *biff Linstrom* (beef patties with capers and beets), and much more. Unlike its fast-food counterparts at Hötorget Square, it's not cheap; expect to spend at least $10. The Saluhall is

FROMMER'S COOL FOR KIDS

RESTAURANTS

Arnold's *(see page 84)* With so many of the trappings of childhood hanging from the ceiling, kids will find it hard to look at their plates.

Coffee House *(see page 75)* There's a high chair, if a toddler is along, as well as down-home atmosphere and plenty of local folks to make kids feel right at home.

NK and PUB cafeterias *(see page 81)* The cafeteria lines let kids see what they're ordering, and the relaxed atmosphere is perfect for small fry.

open on Monday from 10am to 6pm, Tuesday through Friday from 9am to 6pm, and on Saturday from 9am to 3pm. Take the T-Bana to the Östermalmstorg station.

BREAKFAST

Get the day off to an inspiring start at **Strömmen,** Södermalmstorg (tel. 43-44-70), with its breathtaking view of Stockholm Harbor. The doors open for breakfast (choose from light to hearty) at 7:30am Monday through Saturday, at 9am on Sunday. Take the T-Bana to Slussen station on Södermalm.

LATE-NIGHT EATERIES

Slim pickings here. If you're really starving, check out the couple of places in **Kungshallen** that are open until 4am (see "Fast-Food Choices," above).

PICNIC FARE & WHERE TO EAT IT

The **Saluhall** (see "Dining Complex," above), the equivalent of a gourmet deli, displays and sells all manner of fresh, tempting foods. Fruits, vegetables, and a variety of other picnic supplies are also available (and cheaper) at the **outdoor market on Hötorget Square.** It's open year round, Monday through Friday from 9am to 6pm, and on Saturday until 4pm.

Picnic staples may also be purchased at the **supermarket** in the basement of the Åhléns department store, Klarabergsgatan 60 (tel.

24-60-00), at the T-Centralen subway stop. Alternatively, **ICA** is one of the largest supermarket chains around.

Stockholm is filled with restful green pockets in which to enjoy a picnic. My favorite spots are the centrally located **Kungsträdgården,** anywhere on **Djurgården,** and the somewhat secluded **cliffs of Södermalm** overlooking Stockholm Harbor.

---

5. WORTH THE EXTRA BUCKS

NORRMALM

LE BISTROT DE WASAHOF, Dalagatan 46. Tel. 32-34-40.
   Cuisine: SWEDISH. **Reservations:** Suggested. **T-Bana:** Odenplan.
$ Prices: 65–160 Kr ($11.80–$29.10). AE, DC, EU, MC, V.
   Open: Daily 5pm–1am.

This bubbling bistro, not tremendously above budget range, is recommended for a special night out. Just south of Odengatan, the restaurant is in the theater area justifiably known as Stockholm's "off Broadway." The crowd is arty; the food, outstanding; and the atmosphere, convivial. The paintings, which date from 1943, depict the life of eighteenth-century Swedish musician Carl Michael Bellman. The menu changes monthly. Posters from the area's small theaters line the doorway. The restaurant is 2 blocks from the T-Bana stop.

A SUPER SPLURGE

KUNGSHOLMEN

STADSHUSKÄLLAREN [City Hall Cellar], Stadhuset, Kungsholmen. Tel. 50-54-54.
   Cuisine: SWEDISH. **T-Bana:** T-Centralen (a 5-min. walk). **Bus:** 62, which leaves you right outside.
$ Prices: 709.50 Kr ($129) per person, all inclusive. **Reservations:** Required at least 2 days in advance.
   Open: Mon–Fri 11:30am–11:30pm, Sat 2–11:30pm. **Closed:** Sunday.

You don't have to be a Nobel Prize winner, or even the significant other of one, to sit down to an authentic Nobel dinner. The restaurant that orchestrates the prestigious banquet each year can also arrange Nobel dinners for individuals—your choice of any Nobel menu since the first, in 1905. Imagine dining (as laureates actually did in 1989) on appetizers of quail eggs and smoked-eel and sole pâté, followed by a main course of tender moose in a berry sauce (game is almost always a certainty on the menu), and the perennial Nobel dessert, ice cream enveloped in spun sugar, plus petits fours. Fine champagne, wine, and after-dinner drinks accompany the meal. Granted, you pay mightily for the experience, but it is unforgettable, foodwise and otherwise. The cellar restaurant in City Hall looks much as it did when it opened in 1922, and the service and food were never better.

CHAPTER 6

WHAT TO SEE & DO IN STOCKHOLM

- **SUGGESTED ITINERARIES**
- **DID YOU KNOW . . . ?**
1. **THE TOP ATTRACTIONS**
2. **MORE ATTRACTIONS**
- **FROMMER'S FAVORITE STOCKHOLM EXPERIENCES**
3. **COOL FOR KIDS**
4. **SPECIAL-INTEREST SIGHTSEEING**
5. **ORGANIZED TOURS**
6. **SPORTS & RECREATION**
7. **SPECIAL & FREE EVENTS**

Stockholm encourages activity with its tempting array of attractions and outings. You can swim and fish in the downtown area, an unusual feature/accomplishment for any city. Or pay a visit to the well-preserved *Vasa*, a gem of a man-of-war, scooped up out of the depths of Stockholm Harbor, which had cradled it for more than three centuries. Each December, the most prestigious accolades in the world, the Nobel Prizes, are awarded in Stockholm, followed by a grand banquet for 1,200 held in the Blue Hall of City Hall. Skansen, an open-air museum, makes you feel as if you've been transported to the Swedish countryside of years past, when actually your feet are firmly planted in the heart of modern Stockholm. Wile away hours in museums housing works of art from antiquity to the present day. Or poke around the nooks and crannies of Gamla Stan (Old Town), an island full of pedestrian streets and medieval houses that compel you to explore. You can also bike or jog through—or balloon over—this city of wonders.

SUGGESTED ITINERARIES

IF YOU HAVE 1 DAY

Day 1: Start your day in Djurgården with a visit to the **Vasa Museum** and the vast outdoor **Skansen folk museum.** Then

❓ DID YOU KNOW . . . ?

- Sweden is the largest neutral country in Europe.
- Stockholm is the largest city in Scandinavia, with a population of 622,000.
- Sweden's Uppsala University, founded in 1477, is the oldest university in Scandinavia.
- Stockholm is a youthful city: More than 40% of its citizens are 20 to 44 years old.
- According to a 1980 succession act, the first child of the monarch, whether boy or girl, is heir to the throne.
- Queen Christina, who reigned in the 17th century, was actually crowned *king* of Sweden.
- Both Greta Garbo and Ingrid Bergman were students at Stockholm's Royal Theater Dramatic School.
- The water around Stockholm is so clean that people swim and fish in the city center.

set your sights on **Gamla Stan (Old Town)** for an afternoon stroll. Take your time wandering around Stockholm's oldest streets and admiring the city's pretty port views. With few exceptions, Stockholm's best sights are found outdoors.

IF YOU HAVE 2 DAYS

Day 1: Spend the first day as outlined above.

Day 2: On the second day, explore the streets of modern Stockholm's Norrmalm district. A visit to **Kungsträdgården** park is a must and in winter might even include an ice-skating session. During summer, keep an eye out for regularly scheduled special events here. It's easy to go from Norrmalm to Kungsholmen and tour the renowned **City Hall.**

IF YOU HAVE 3 DAYS

Days 1–2: Spend the first two days as outlined above.

Day 3: Make the short trip to **Drottningholm Palace** and take in the Swedish royal couple's house and gardens. Later, back in Stockholm's Old Town, compare it with the older **Royal Palace** and visit **Stockholm Cathedral (Storkyrkan),** the city's oldest building.

IF YOU HAVE 5 OR MORE DAYS

Days 1–3: Spend the first three days as outlined above.

Day 4: Continue museum-hopping at the **Millesgården,** the **Museum of National Antiquities,** the **National Museum,** and others. There are plenty from which to choose.

Day 5: Consider an archipelago cruise or a trip to any one of the many islands around the city; **Mariefred** is delightful.

1. THE TOP ATTRACTIONS

DJURGÅRDEN

Many of Stockholm's best sights are clustered on or around the island of Djurgården, which is 10 minutes east of Gamla Stan by boat. Djurgården was once a royal deer park, and much of it is still in its natural state. In fact, you may see deer, hare, and rare birds along the wooded paths. The attractions have been designed to integrate gracefully with the thick forests and sweeping harbor views.

HOW TO GET TO DJURGÅRDEN

The most enjoyable way to *reach* Djurgården is by ferry from Gamla Stan (see "By Ferry" in Section 2 of Chapter 3). Otherwise, take the tram that picks up passengers near Sweden House. Bus no. 47 from Central Station or Norrmalmstorg is another alternative. Bus no. 69 goes all the way to the tip of the island.

VASA MUSEUM (Vasamuseet). Tel. 666-048-00.
When the warship *Vasa* set sail on its maiden voyage in August of 1628, it was heralded as the pride of the Swedish fleet. But before it even reached the mouth of Stockholm Harbor, the 64-cannon man-of-war caught a sudden gust of wind, lurched to one side, and sank to the bottom of the sea. Forgotten for centuries, the boat was located in 1956 by marine archeologist Anders Franzén, who raised national interest in the wreck and was able to raise the warship from the depths of the harbor. Today, the highly ornamented, well-preserved wooden vessel is the most frequently visited attraction in Stockholm.

It took 5 years and advanced technology to raise the fragile ship intact, but in 1961 the *Vasa* was successfully reclaimed and housed in a climatically controlled museum. In the summer of 1990, the *Vasa* moved into a stunning new $27-million building, marking the latest chapter in this ship's long history.

When you visit, be sure to see the carvings on the bow and stern and the life-size replica of the ship's interior. Children love the computer area, where they can try their hand at raising the *Vasa*. Two original masts and two copies will be added by 1995.

Admission: 25 Kr ($4.55) for adults, 5 Kr (90¢) for children under 16.

Open: Summer, daily 9:30am–7pm; winter, daily 10am–5pm (to 8pm on Wed). **Closed:** Dec 24–26, Jan 1. **Directions:** See "How to Get to Djurgården," above.

SKANSEN. Tel. 663-05-00.

The year 1991 marked the 100th anniversary of this 75-acre outdoor museum. Home to more than 150 buildings from the 16th to the early 20th century, Skansen displays traditional Nordic log cabins and stone houses in a pastoral setting. Weather-beaten and imperfect, yet thoroughly winsome, many of them were transported from locations all across Sweden. Some of the buildings (which are divided into rural dwellings and 18th-century town houses) maintain their original interiors, including painted wooden walls, fireplaces, spinning wheels, old plates, and assorted folk decor. Throughout the museum, craftspeople, using traditional tools and methods, demonstrate the former ways of farming, metalworking, glassblowing, typesetting, bookbinding, and more than a dozen other trades.

Though the museum's buildings are interesting in and of themselves, Skansen's real success stems from its exceptionally peaceful setting on a tree-lined peninsula replete with wooden bridges and stone walls. And there is a small but particularly endearing zoo with a farmlike setting and a modern aquarium.

Restaurants and food stands are scattered throughout the grounds; but if the weather is nice, it's more enjoyable to pack a picnic. During spring and summer, try folk dancing with the locals; dances are scheduled every evening during the week at 7pm, and on Sunday at 2:30 and 4pm. A map of Skansen, sold at the entrance, will definitely come in handy. There is also a nice gift shop on the premises.

Admission: May–Aug, 24 Kr ($4.35) for adults, 9 Kr ($1.65) for children; Sept–Apr, 16 Kr ($2.90) for adults, 5 Kr (90¢) for children.

Open: Museum grounds, May–Aug, daily 9am–10pm; Sept–Apr, daily 9am–5pm. Historic houses, May–Aug, daily 11am–5pm; Sept–Apr, daily 11am–3pm. **Directions:** See "How to Get to Djurgården," above.

IMPRESSIONS

The waters are great and deep about this city, [which is] pleasant and noble for the situation; and the grounds about it are dry and wholesome, yet fruitful. The streets are some of them large, others more narrow; most of them straight . . . Taken altogether, from the prospect of the mountains upon the churches, castle, houses, waters and ships, the town appears noble and beautiful.
—BULSTRODE WHITELOCKE
(JOURNAL OF THE SWEDISH EMBASSY IN 1653 AND 1654, PUBLISHED 1855)

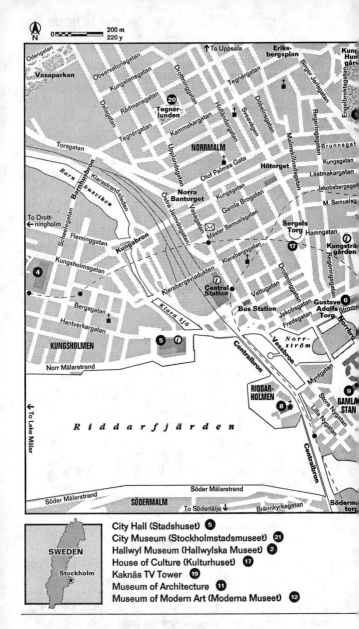

City Hall (Stadshuset)	**5**
City Museum (Stockholmstadsmuseet)	**21**
Hallwyl Museum (Hallwylska Museet)	**2**
House of Culture (Kulturhuset)	**17**
Kaknäs TV Tower	**19**
Museum of Architecture	**11**
Museum of Modern Art (Moderna Museet)	**12**

GAMLA STAN [OLD TOWN]

Along the cobblestoned lanes and alleys of Gamla Stan, striking medieval buildings blush pretty shades of pastel. Black wrought-iron streetlamps sprout from the squat buildings to illuminate the store-

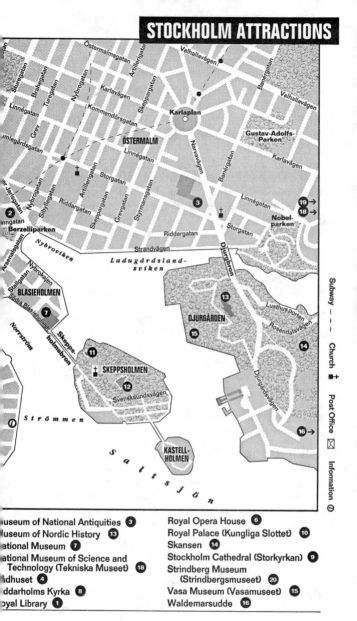

STOCKHOLM ATTRACTIONS

Östermalmsgatan · Valhallavägen

Sturegatan · Brahegatan · Tureg · Nybrogatan · Karlavägen · Banérgatan · Valhallavägen

Linnégatan · Grev · Tuegatan · Kommendörsgatan · Skeppargatan · **Karlaplan** · Narvavägen · **Gustav-Adolfs-Parken**

mlegårdsgatan · **ÖSTERMALM** · Linnégatan · Karlavägen

ar Jargatan · Nybrogatan · Styrlegatan · Artillerigatan · Storgatan · Skeppargatan · Grevgatan · Styrmansgatan · Linnégatan · **19 →** · **18 →** · **Nobel-parken**

2 · nngatan · **Berzeliiparken** · Riddargatan · **3** · Storgatan

Arsenalegatan · Nybroviken · Strandvägen · Riddargatan · Djurgårdsbron

Skallgatan · Södra Blasieholmst · Nybrokajen · *Ladugårdsland-sviken*

BLASIEHOLMEN · **7** · Skepps- holmsbron · **13** · Lusthusporten

Norrström · **DJURGÅRDEN** · Rosendalsvägen

11 · **SKEPPSHOLMEN** · **15** · **14**

12 · Svensksundsvägen · Djurgårdsvägen

17 · *Strömmen* · **16 →**

S a l t s j ö n · **KASTELL-HOLMEN**

Subway – – – Church ╬ Post Office ⊠ Information ⍟

useum of National Antiquities **3**	Royal Opera House **6**
useum of Nordic History **13**	Royal Palace (Kungliga Slottet) **10**
ational Museum **7**	Skansen **14**
ational Museum of Science and Technology (Tekniska Museet) **18**	Stockholm Cathedral (Storkyrkan) **9**
ådhuset **4**	Strindberg Museum (Strindbergsmuseet) **20**
ddarholms Kyrka **8**	Vasa Museum (Vasamuseet) **15**
oyal Library **1**	Waldemarsudde **16**

fronts below. And high above some houses, metal hooks from long-ago days hang over garret windows, still ready to hoist up cargo.

Getting lost in Gamla Stan's timeless maze of car-free streets is one of Stockholm's greatest pleasures. This is the city's most heavily touristed area, and although you may glimpse a contemporary office interior or pass a store window displaying haute couture, Gamla Stan's quiet, historical charm stoically maintains an authentic ancient atmosphere.

ROYAL PALACE [Kungliga Slottet], off Skeppsbron. Tel. 789-85-00.

Although a royal residence has stood on this spot in Gamla Stan for more than 700 years, the current building dates only from the 17th century. In the 17th and 18th centuries, Sweden flourished as one of Europe's major powers; and this grand palace, filled with more than 600 rooms, was rebuilt to reflect this status. Although you may find the massive stone facade of this huge complex somewhat uninspired, the 18th-century royal apartment interiors are as grand and distinguished as any with their Swedish baroque, Louis XVI, and Empire-style furnishings. Flamboyantly painted ceilings, opulent chandeliers, and lush tapestries are on permanent display. The crown jewels may be viewed in the palace vaults, along with other trappings of royalty, such as coronation clothes and gilded parade coaches. Note that the apartments and other exhibits may close without notice as the palace is used for official state functions on special occasions. King Carl XVI Gustaf only performs ceremonial tasks here; he and the Queen and their children reside at Drottningholm Palace (see Chapter 10, Section 1). At noon (1pm on Sunday) you can see the Changing of the Guard in the palace courtyard. During summer, the spectacle also includes the guards' parade and music.

Admission: 25 Kr ($4.55) for adults, 5 Kr (90¢) for students and children under 16.

Open: May–Aug, Tues–Sat 10am–3pm, Sun noon–3pm; Sept–Apr, Tues–Sun noon–3pm. **T-Bana:** Gamla Stan.

STOCKHOLM CATHEDRAL [Storkyrkan], Trångsund (next to Royal Palace). Tel. 723-30-00.

Since the 13th century, this church has been the backdrop for Sweden's most important religious ceremonies, including coronations and royal marriages. The city's oldest existing building, it contains the oldest known painting of Stockholm (1535), which portrays little more than a sleepy hamlet, and a large wooden sculpture of St. George battling the dragon, installed in 1489. Every Saturday at 1pm, and on Sunday once or twice a month, there are concerts featuring the church's huge 18th-century organ.

Admission: Free.

Open: Daily 9am–5pm (until 4pm in winter). **T-Bana:** Gamla Stan.

KUNGSHOLMEN

CITY HALL (Stadshuset), Hantverkargatan 1. Tel. 785-90-00.

Stockholm's landmark City Hall, designed by Ragnar Östberg in National Romantic style, is home to the annual Nobel Prize banquet and may be visited by guided tour only. The tour's highlight is undoubtedly the Golden Hall, lavishly decorated with more than 19 million 23-karat-gold tiles—it's one of the world's most beautiful rooms. Dinners honoring Nobel Prize winners were originally held in the Golden Hall, but the swelling guest list has forced the party to relocate to the much larger Blue Hall, which isn't blue. Marble floors, stone columns, and Gothic motifs throughout make City Hall look and feel much older than its 69 years. In summer only, you may climb—without the group tour—to the top of the distinctive tower, which is topped by three gleaming crowns, the symbol of Sweden and the national coat-of-arms.

Admission: 20 Kr ($3.65) for adults, free for children under 13.

Open: Tours—summer, daily at 10am, 11am, noon, and 2pm; the rest of the year, daily at 10am and noon. Tower visits—May–Sept, daily 10am–3pm. **T-Bana:** Rådhuset.

NORRMALM & SKEPPSHOLMEN

NATIONAL MUSEUM, Blasieholhamnen. Tel. 666-42-50.

Although it displays masterpieces by stars like Rembrandt, Rubens, and El Greco, this pleasant and manageable museum is not labyrinthine. The collection is well marked (in Swedish), and there are tours available during summer. Be sure to visit the ground-floor gallery of paintings by Swedish modern masters from the mid-19th to mid-20th century, including Anders Zorn and Carl Larsson; it's to the left, just inside the entrance. The second-floor Department of Applied Arts features more than 28,000 pieces of porcelain, glassware, silverwork, and jewelry, including a contemporary Swedish design gallery. The third floor houses works by Renoir, Degas, Rodin, and Corot, along with 16th- and 17th-century French, Italian, Flemish, and Dutch painters. The museum is located at the foot of the bridge to Skeppsholmen.

Admission: 30 Kr ($5.45) for adults, 15 Kr ($2.70) for students and seniors, free for children under 16; free for everyone on Fri.

Open: July–Aug, Tues–Sun 10am–5pm; Sept–June, Tues 10am–9pm, Wed–Sun 10am–5pm. **T-Bana:** Kungsträdgården.

MUSEUM OF MODERN ART (Moderna Museet), Skeppsholmen. Tel. 666-42-50.

Open late four times a week, and an excellent choice for an evening of museum going, the Museum of Modern Art houses the country's largest collection of 20th-century paintings by Swedish and international artists. Featured are works by Picasso, Matisse, Dalí, Warhol, Ernst, Kandinsky, Braque, Miró, and Pollock. Although the temporary exhibitions often lack star power, they are usually adventurous and tackle unusual themes. The pleasant museum cafe offers a variety of dishes under 49 Kr ($8.90), and there are a museum shop and a playful sculpture garden. Housed in the same building, the small Museum of Photography mounts outstanding special exhibits.

Admission: 30 Kr ($5.45) for adults, 20 Kr ($3.65) for students and seniors; free to all on Thurs.

Open: Tues–Fri 11am–9pm, Sat–Sun 11am–5pm. **T-Bana:** Kunsträdgården. **Bus:** 65 to Skeppsholmen.

2. MORE ATTRACTIONS

DJURGÅRDEN

WALDEMARSUDDE, Prins Eugens Väg 6. Tel. 662-18-33.

This brilliant palace was once the residence of Prince Eugen (1865–1947) and was donated to the city upon his death. It's famous not only for its glorious architecture and truly palatial views, but for the artwork of Prince Eugen himself. The "artist prince," as Eugen is now known, was a prolific landscape painter—he did the murals at City Hall—and some say that he was pretty facile, too. Although the palace has a fine collection of paintings by modern Nordic masters, these are, by far, outnumbered by the prince's own works. On the third floor, Eugen outdid himself with some frescoes. Nestled in a forest, the palace overlooks the port and Old Town. Having a picnic here or lingering to watch the sun set is perfectly acceptable; in fact, the locals do it all the time.

Admission: 20 Kr ($3.65) for adults, 10 Kr ($1.80) for students and seniors, free for children under 16.

Open: June–Aug, Tues and Thurs 11am–5pm and 7–9pm, Wed and Fri–Sun 11am–5pm; Sept–Nov 26 and Dec 26–May, Tues–Sun 11am–4pm. **Closed:** Nov 20–Dec 26. **Bus:** 47.

THIEL GALLERY [Thielska Galleriet], Sjötullsbacken 6-8. Tel. 662-58-84.

This gallery was built to house the burgeoning collection of banker and art patron Ernst Thiel. When Thiel went bankrupt in 1924, the Swedish government purchased the gallery and opened it to the public. Here you'll see paintings by Gauguin, Vuillard, Anders Zorn, Carl Wilhelmson, and Ernst Josephson. One room is exclusively devoted to Carl Larsson. Climb to the tower room to see the two dozen works by Edvard Munch and a fine view of the archipelago.

FROMMER'S FAVORITE

STOCKHOLM EXPERIENCES

Standing Near the Water and Gazing at the City Stockholm is breathtakingly beautiful and never more so than when seen from the water's edge (since there's so much water, that's much of the time). All you have to do is stand still—the views encompass you.

A Bike Ride Around Djurgården The island is fun for walking or jogging, too, but you see so much more of it on a bike.

Half a Day at Skansen You're in the heart of the city, but it feels like the country. You'll admire flaxen-haired Swedish children; they're here en masse.

Museum Visits on Free Day The Museum of Modern Art and the National Museum are free to the public on Thursday and Friday, respectively.

Exploring Gamla Stan [Old Town] Some of the most charming streets in Europe are tucked away on this small island.

A Ferry Ride The Stockholm archipelago, chockablock with 24,000 islands, keeps the city's ferries bustling. A ride on one promises a quick, fun getaway without going far away.

On the grounds are sculptures by Rodin and Norwegian artist Gustav Vigeland; Thiel is buried beneath Rodin's *Shadow*.

Admission: 20 Kr ($3.65) for adults, 10 Kr ($1.80) for students and seniors.

Open: Mon–Sat noon–4pm, Sun 1–4pm. **Bus:** 69.

MUSEUM OF NORDIC HISTORY [Nordiska Museet], Djurgårdsvägen 6-16, Djurgården. Tel. 22-41-20.

Located in an impressive stone building, this ethnographic museum documents changes in Nordic life from 500 years ago to present day. You'll learn how Swedes in the past lived, dressed, hunted, and fished. There are more than a million objects housed here, and it's fascinating to see how Scandinavian culture has evolved. Don't miss the grandfather clock collection. The museum's cafe offers a daily lunch special.

Admission: 20 Kr ($3.65) for adults, free for children under 16.

Open: June–Aug, Mon–Wed and Fri 10am–4pm, Thurs 10am–

8pm, Sat–Sun noon–5pm; Sept–May, Tues, Wed, and Fri 10am–8pm, Sat–Sun 11am–4pm. **Bus:** 47 or 69, or take ferry from Gamla Stan to Djurgården.

NORRMALM

HALLWYL MUSEUM [Hallwylska Museet], Hamngatan 4. Tel. 666-44-75.

Considered Stockholm's most unique (perhaps most eccentric) museum, this magnificent turn-of-the-century private residence is filled with 70 years' worth of collecting by Countess Wilhelmina von Hallwyl. Everything from buttons to Dutch and Swedish paintings, to European china and Chinese ceramics, to silver and weapons is on display. Admission to the house is by guided tour only. Arrive early; they book up quickly.

Admission: 30 Kr ($5.45).

Open: Tues–Sun noon–3pm; tour in English at 1pm, in Swedish at noon and 2pm; off-season, English tour is on Sunday only. **T-Bana:** Kungsträdgården.

HOUSE OF CULTURE [Kulturhuset], Sergels Torg 3. Tel. 700-01-00.

This modern building, a tribute to 1960s architecture, houses exhibits that enlighten Swedes about other cultures, thus the name. On its multiple floors, you will discover numerous galleries, stages, cafes, a large library, a bookshop, thousands of records (which you may listen to with headsets), 30 daily newspapers, more than 50 magazines, and chess boards. The obelisk-like glass sculpture outside, particularly striking at night, is by Edvin Ohrström.

Admission: Free.

Open: Information, Tues–Fri 11am–6pm, Sat 11am–2pm. **T-Bana:** T-Centralen.

LIDINGÖ

MILLESGÅRDEN, Carl Milles Väg 2. Tel. 731-50-60.

Often referred to as one of the greatest Swedish artists, sculptor Carl Milles (1875–1955) returned to Stockholm late in life and designed this garden that sits high on a hill on the island of Lidingö. The Milles Garden is a little difficult to get to, but those who are eager enough will be rewarded with views of magnificent fountains and sculptures overlooking all of Stockholm. This breathtaking site beautifully augments some of Milles's best-known and dramatic works, based on mythological themes.

Admission: 25 Kr ($4.55) for adults, free for children under 12.

Open: May–Sept, daily 10am–5pm; Oct–Apr, Tues–Sun 11am–4pm. **T-Bana:** Ropsten; then bus to Torsvik. Trips take about 20 minutes.

PANORAMAS

Located on Södermalm just over the bridge from Gamla Stan, the **Katarina Elevator** lifts visitors to a perch high above Stockholm. If you're feeling strong, climb the **Södermalm cliffs** yourself; just don't miss the opportunity to see the spectacular view. Admission is 3 Kr (55¢), and the elevator is open Monday through Saturday from 7:30am to 10pm; take the T-Bana to Slussen. The view from **Strömmen** restaurant, on Södermalmstorg opposite the T-Bana exit, is equally enthralling, just not as high. From the **City Hall Tower,** you can see Kungsholmen, Gamla Stan, and Långholmen. The **Kaknäs TV Tower,** on Djurgården, Scandinavia's highest structure, provides a different bird's-eye view of the city and environs. For a compelling glimpse of the archipelago, climb to the tower room of the **Thiel Gallery,** also on Djurgården.

PARKS

Parks are one of Stockholm's loveliest assets. Among the city's most popular green spots are **Kungsträdgården** in Norrmalm, a bustling urban park and the city's summer gathering spot, and the entire islands of **Djurgården,** including the **Skansen** open-air museum, and **Skeppsholmen. Waldemarsudde** and **Millesgården** are also excellent strolling grounds.

Tanto Lunden, with tiny cottages and carefully tended gardens near the city center, is a special Stockholm phenomenon. It was created in 1919 so that city workers who couldn't afford a country home could benefit from country living just the same. The cottages, one room each, look more like dollhouses; their equally tiny yards are filled with birdhouses and compost heaps. To get here, take bus no. 43 or the T-Bana to Zinkensdamm. Zinkens Väg—where Touristgården Zinken youth hostel is located—dead-ends into Tanto Lunden; climb the wooden steps and enter a world in miniature. Don't overlook delightful house no. 69.

SUBWAY ART

Stockholm claims to have the longest art gallery in the world: its own subway system. Many of the 99 stations contain commissioned original artwork, much of it extra-large in format. Stations of particular note, which are used frequently by out-of-towners on their sightseeing excursions, are T-Centralen, Kungsträdgården, and Slussen.

3. COOL FOR KIDS

TOP CITY ATTRACTIONS

Look under "The Top Attractions" and "More Attractions," above, for the following:

Vasa Museum   (*see page 92*) As swashbuckling a place as kids are likely to find outside of the TV screen, the warship *Vasa* is so real their imaginations will set sail the moment they step inside the museum. The computer area draws children like ships draw seagulls.

Skansen   (*see page 93*) The lanes, old houses, and people in period costumes lead kids into another world. The zoo is particularly popular with local children and provides an icebreaker (as if kids need one) for meeting them.

Museum of Nordic History   (*see page 99*) After seeing where the Swedes lived at Skansen, kids can learn how they lived, dressed, hunted, and fished at this museum. The grandfather clock collection is always a big hit.

TWO MUSEUMS & A TOWER

MARIONETTE MUSEUM (Marionettmuseet), Brunnsgatan 6. Tel. 117-112.
This enchanting, award-winning museum displays 1,000 puppets—string puppets, shadow puppets, glove puppets, even battery-driven puppets—from around the world. Sweden and Asia are particularly well represented. Children may play with some of the puppets. Ask at the desk for exhibit descriptions in English. There is free coffee for visitors, and you may even sit and have tea in the Japanese room.

Admission: 15 Kr ($2.70) for adults, 5 Kr (90¢) for kids. On weekends, 5 Kr (90¢) for adults and kids, including performance at adjacent Puppet Theater.

IMPRESSIONS

Swedish children always look as if they were the offspring of the moon rather than of the sun, and it takes them some time to be done brown—several summers.
—KATHLEEN NOTT
(*A CLEAN, WELL-LIGHTED PLACE*, 1961)

Open: Tues–Sun 1–4pm. **Closed:** Mid-June–mid-Aug. **T-Bana:** Hötorget.

NATIONAL MUSEUM OF SCIENCE AND TECHNOLOGY [Tekniska Museet], Museivägen 7, Djurgården. Tel. 663-10-85.

The hands-on exhibits encourage kids to experiment to their hearts' content. On display are steam engines, aircraft, and vintage cars.

Admission: 25 Kr ($4.55) for adults, 10 Kr ($1.80) for children.
Open: Mon–Fri 10am–4pm, Sat–Sun noon–4pm. **Bus:** 69.

KAKNÄS TV TOWER. Tel. 789-24-35.

Within walking distance of the National Museum of Science and Technology, this 155-meter (169.5-ft.) tower provides a panoramic view of Stockholm and the archipelago.

Admission: 15 Kr ($2.70) for adults, 8 Kr ($1.45) for children 7 and older.
Open: May–Aug, daily 9am–midnight; Apr–Sept, daily 9am–10pm; Oct–Mar, daily 9am–6pm. **Bus:** 69.

---

4. SPECIAL-INTEREST SIGHTSEEING

FOR THE LITERARY ENTHUSIAST

Admirers of Swedish dramatist August Strindberg (1849–1912) can visit the **Strindberg Museum (Strindbergsmuseet),** Drottninggatan 85 (tel. 11-37-89), a reconstruction of his last home, built on its original site. The house, filled with authentic furniture and details, includes a replica of the author's library. The museum is open Tuesday through Friday from 10am to 4pm (on Tuesday also from 6 to 8pm), and on Saturday and Sunday from noon to 5pm. Admission is 15 Kr ($2.70) for adults, free for children under 16. Take the T-Bana to Rådmansgatan.

FOR THE HISTORY BUFF

Stockholm was founded in the 13th century, and despite the fancy boutiques that now line the streets of **Gamla Stan,** you still get a sense of what it must have been like here hundreds of years ago. Cars are banned from most streets, and the area's narrow alleyways retain their ancient charm. Wander along Österlånggatan and Västerlånggatan, following the path where the ancient city walls once stood.

Those interested in the Vikings and early Swedish history will enjoy a visit to the **Museum of National Antiquities,** Narvavägen 13–17 (tel. 783-94-00). Viking stone inscriptions, 10th-century coins, and ancient armor are displayed here. The collection, which complements that of the Museum of Nordic History, shows daily life from the first dawn of time to the Middle Ages. The museum shop is worth a visit for its fine collection of English-language history books. The museum itself is open Tuesday through Sunday from noon to 5pm (in winter, on Thursday until 7pm). Admission is 20 Kr ($3.65) for adults; 15 Kr ($2.70) for students, seniors, and children under 16. To get there, take the T-Bana to Karlaplan or bus no. 44, 47, or 69.

Next in the historical chain of progression is **Skansen,** which shows how the Swedes have lived (and in what kinds of structures) over the past 400 years, and the **Museum of Nordic History,** which details how Sweden became a modern society (see Section 1 and Section 2 of this chapter, respectively).

FOR THE ARCHITECTURE LOVER

Stockholm's most stunning edifices line the water; the waterfront is extensive and the gorgeous buildings are plentiful. Most were erected around the turn of the century and are maintained in excellent condition. The city's picture-postcard beauty is most typified by the view from the Djurgårdsbron, the Beaux Arts bridge connecting Djurgården—where Skansen and the Vasa Museum are located—to the rest of the city.

MUSEUM OF ARCHITECTURE [Arkitekturmuseet], Skeppsholmen. Tel. 11-75-10.

This small museum has models, maps, and architectural plans of Stockholm. Some films in English are shown, and special exhibits in summer have English and Swedish texts.

Admission: 15 Kr ($2.70) for adults, 10 Kr ($1.80) for children.

Open: Tues 11am–9pm, Wed–Sun 11am–5pm. **T-Bana:** Kunsträdgården. **Bus:** 65.

STOCKHOLM CITY MUSEUM [Stockholmstadsmuseet], Södermalmstorg, Slussen. Tel. 700-05-00.

Located near the subway exit, the City Museum depicts Stockholm in centuries past in drawings and models. Texts are in Swedish only, but visitors should still find the first and second floors well done and interesting. The museum also has a good cafe.

Admission: 15 Kr ($2.70) for adults, free for children under 18.

Open: Tues–Thurs 11am–7pm (to 9pm Jan to mid-May), Fri–Mon 11am–5pm.

5. ORGANIZED TOURS

Some visitors find Stockholm a difficult city to negotiate initially because of all the islands and the sights spread out on them. A tour can save you a lot of time and be quite informative as well.

Stockholm Sightseeing (tel. 11-11-42) offers the least expensive panoramic tour of the city. Buses leave from in front of Sweden House, and tours take 2½ hours and cost 145 Kr ($26.35), half price for children, from mid-May through September. From October through mid-May, tours are scaled back to 1½ hours and cost 135 Kr ($24.55) for adults, half price for children.

The company offers an "Under the Bridges of Stockholm" tour from May through September. It takes 1½ hours and costs 95 Kr ($17.30) for adults, half price for children. The boat leaves from in front of the ticket booth opposite the Grand Hotel.

A similar but shorter (1-hour) water tour, "Cityringen," is offered from late April through September by **Strömma's Sightseeing** (tel. 23-33-75) and costs 65 Kr ($11.80) for adults, half price for children ages 6 to 11. The sleek glass-enclosed boat leaves from City Hall and Nybroviken, which is opposite the Royal Dramatic Theater.

Visit the **Stockholm Information Service** (see "Tourist Information" in Section 1 of Chapter 3) for tour times and reservations, and refer to the "Sightseeing" section of *Stockholm This Week* for a full list of tour operators.

6. SPORTS & RECREATION

Stockholm's natural beauty makes it a shoo-in for outdoor sports, jogging, fishing, and swimming right in the downtown area. If you choose to be a spectator instead, you won't be disappointed.

IMPRESSIONS

Noble, nude and far more modern than any other people in Europe, they sport in the icy waters of the Baltic, they roam naked in the primeval forest.
—ALDOUS HUXLEY
(ALONG THE ROAD, 1925)

SPECTATOR SPORTS

For ice hockey, basketball, and tennis (not to mention the occasional rock concert), check upcoming events at the **Stockholm Globe Arena (Globen)**, Johanneshov (tel. 600-34-00 for information, 10-88-00 for tickets), just south of the downtown area and less than 10 minutes from Central Station. At 85 meters (1,115 ft.), it's the highest spherical construction in the world and can seat up to 16,000 people.

National soccer games are played at **Råsunda Football Stadium**, Solnavägen 55 (tel. 835-09-00 for information, 83-25-25 for tickets); international teams compete at the **Stadion**, Valhallavägen/ Lidingövägen (tel. 21-94-56), a striking red-brick building set in a ring of trees. Built in 1912 for the Olympic Games, it is also the site for summer pop and rock concerts—David Bowie performed here in 1990.

Horse racing occurs at **Täby Galopp** (756-3230), half an hour from Stockholm by train; trotting races, at **Solvalla**, Tegelviksg 22 (tel. 28-93-60), one of the world's largest arenas for the sport. Check with the Swedish Information Service for events and dates.

RECREATION

Aerobics **Friskis & Svettis**, a name synonymous with aerobics in Stockholm, organizes sessions—free to all—in the city parks during the summer. Inquire at Sweden House.

Ballooning Glide right over downtown Stockholm's spires, parks, and squares; dawn or dusk is the best time. You might even get champagne when you land. The sport is popular all over Sweden. In Stockholm, contact **Aventyrsresor** (tel. 54-11-55) or **STF** (tel. 790-32-00). Expect to pay about $100 for the hourlong thrill.

Bicycle Rentals From April through September, bikes are available for hire from **Skepp o Hoj**, on Djurgården (tel. 660-57-57). Two Baltic islands offer tempting biking getaways: **Gotland**— 112 miles long, 31 miles wide, scenic, flat, and filled with orchids—is crisscrossed with a network of trails (for more information, call Gotland's Tourist Service, 0498-490-50); and **Öland** has bike paths that cut through a pretty landscape of forests, beaches, and fields of wildflowers (for more information, call the Öland Tourist Office, 0485-123-40). To get to either, you'd have to plan an excursion out of Stockholm. For information about biking around Stockholm, as well as farther afield, contact **Svenska Cykelsällskapet**, Box 6006, S-164 06 Kista, Sweden (tel. 45/8-751-62-04).

Boat Rentals Check with the Stockholm Information Service for information on renting watercraft (tel. 789-20-00).

Canoeing In summer, you can rent canoes just over the bridge on the island of Djurgården. The rental place is to your right.

Fishing It's perfectly permissible in the city center—no permit required—and you might just haul in a salmon for your efforts.

Golf Stockholm has 20 golf courses, none more than 30 kilometers (18½ miles) from the city. Golf tournaments are held regularly.

Ice Skating It only costs 10 Kr ($1.80) to rent skates from Sweden House and skate right out front, in Kungsträdgården. Impromptu rinks pop up all over the archipelago once the water freezes.

Jogging Some of the most scenic jogging in the world is along the shoreline paths of Djurgården and on the small island of Skeppsholmen.

Skiing Stockholm is not known for its ski facilities, but it does have them—some 30 downhill slopes in its environs. Most slopes are set up for night skiing, in case you're too busy sightseeing during the day, and they are accessible by public transportation. Inquire at the Swedish Information Service at Sweden House.

Swimming Hard as it is to believe in these days of rampant urban pollution, the water around Stockholm is clean enough to swim in, and there are two downtown beaches to prove it. **Smedsuddsbadet** is at Mariebergsparken (tel. 785-83-55), accessible by T-Bana to Fridhemsplan, or bus no. 40, 54, 56, or 57 to Västerbroplan. **Långholmsbadet,** a rocky beach on Långholmen, is reached via T-Bana to Hornstull, bus no. 40 to Högalidsgatan, or no. 66 to Bergsunds Strand.

Badet means swimming facilities in Swedish. **Forsgrenskabadet** is a modern, tiled indoor swimming complex on Södermalm, Medborgarplatsen 2-4 (tel. 40-11-02). It has three pools, a cafe, sparkling-clean changing rooms, and a sauna. Only three stops from Central Station. If you've left your swimsuit at home, don't fret; they'll rent you one for 8 Kr ($1.45).

7. SPECIAL & FREE EVENTS

During the summer, **Kungsträdgården**—Norrmalm's park, adjacent to Sweden House—comes alive almost daily with classical-music concerts, rock bands, theater performances, and various other attractions. During the winter, an outdoor ice rink opens up here, providing some of the best (and least expensive) inner-city skating anywhere.

Summertime also means frequent free and almost-free concerts in other parts of Stockholm. **Sommarnättskonserter (Summer Night Concerts)** are held on the stairs of the National Museum during July and August, and **folk dancing** is performed at Skansen weekday evenings and Sunday afternoons.

CHAPTER 7

STROLLING AROUND STOCKHOLM

Stockholm is such a visually beautiful city that it's a pleasure to walk anywhere in it. Your eyes can't help but fall on graceful buildings, tranquil water, pockets of green, unhurried people, and rosy-cheeked children. And perhaps no city in the world offers more chance to get out and enjoy nature right in the heart of an urban center.

WALKING TOUR 1 — Gamla Stan

Start: Riksbron (bridge connecting Norrmalm and Gamla Stan).
Finish: House of Parliament.
Time: 3 hours.
Best Time: Anytime, day or evening.

Gamla Stan (Old Town), with its maze of narrow medieval streets, can be as confusing as it is enchanting. Newcomers often fear getting lost here and stick almost solely to Västerlånggatan, the main thoroughfare and shopping street. By doing so, they are certain to miss out on some memorable streets, architecture, and squares.

This is your key to unlocking the confusion of Gamla Stan streets, all of which are pedestrian-only on Stadsholmen (City Island), the largest and best known of the drops of land composing the Old Town. To get to the heart of Gamla Stan from Norrmalm, you have to cross two bridges. Begin at:

1. **Riksbron,** which is the small bridge at the end of Norrmalm's pedestrian street Drottninggatan, and walk across onto Helgeands Island. Just beyond the bridge you get a view of City Hall, to your right, and the:

2. **House of Parliament (Riksdagshuset),** Riksgatan 3A, to your left. The cornerstone for it was laid in 1897. You may explore the interior, but only as part of a guided tour. From here, continue to the second bridge:

3. **Stallbron,** which provides the most dramatic entry into Gamla Stan, especially at night. To your right is another view of City Hall and its square tower topped with three crowns. To your left is the city's luxurious Grand Hotel. From here, follow Västerlånggatan; when Gamla Stan was a walled city, Västerlånggatan was the road running along the outside of the wall. When you get to Storkyrkobrinken, turn right and walk one block to:

4. **Riddarhuset (House of Nobility),** Riddarhustorget 10, a palace built for the Swedish nobility in 1657 in Dutch classical style. Behind it is:

5. **Riddar House Square (Riddarhustorget),** with striking twin houses, added in 1870, and a central statue of Axel Oxenstierna, carved in 1890. Axel originally owned this parcel of land. Beyond the square is another view of City Hall, photogenic from every angle.

    From here, walk back to Stora Nygatan, where at the corner of Stora Gråmunkegränd, you'll happen upon:

6. **Stampen,** a winsome combination of a jazz club and pub; you may see performers in the window. If you look inside, you'll notice all manner of memorabilia hanging from the ceiling. They represent hocked items, reminiscent of this building's former incarnation as a pawnshop.

    Continue along Stora Nygatan a few blocks to Gåsgränd and turn left, passing:

7. **Gästorget,** a small square with a small sculpture of boxers, with heads at their feet. Continue along Gåsgränd until you reconnect with the main thoroughfare, Västerlånggatan. Turn right onto it (or left, if you want to backtrack a couple of blocks to browse in the stores you bypassed). The shops along both sides of the street afford plenty to see—and buy, if you're so inclined. When you get to Kåkbrinken, turn left, throw your body into third gear, and walk up the hill to:

8. **Stortorget,** the oldest square in Stockholm. A market is held here at Christmas. It's hard to imagine that this peacefully sloping square surrounded by town houses was the site of a gory moment in Swedish history known as the Stockholm Bloodbath. In 1520, more than 80 prominent citizens were hanged or beheaded here by Christian II, now known as the Tyrant. This Danish ruler feared insurrection in the Kalmar Union of Sweden, Norway, and Denmark. Among the victims in this massacre were the bishop, nobility, councilmen, merchants, and the father of Gustav Vasa, who would become king of Sweden in 1523.

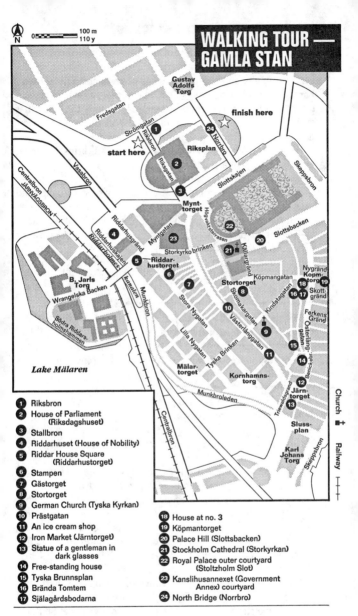

WALKING TOUR — GAMLA STAN

Gustav Adolfs Torg

finish here

Fredsgatan

Strömgatan
start here

Riksplan

Slottskajen

Skeppsbron

Vasabron

Centralbron
JÄRNVÄGSBRON

Riddarhusgränd
Riddarhuskajen
RIDDARHOLMEN

Myntgatan

Myntorget

Högvaktsterrassen

Slottsbacken

B. Jarls Torg

Wrangelska Backen

Riddarhustorget
Riddar-
hustorget

Storkyrko brinken

Kållargränd

Köpmangatan

Stortorget

Nygränd
Köpmantorget

Skottgränd

Munkbron

Stora Nygatan

Lilla Nygatan

Skomakargatan

Västerlånggatan

Kindstagatan

Österlånggatan

Ferkens Gränd

Södra Riddarholmshamnen

Lake Mälaren

Tyska Brinken

Mälartorget

Kornhamnstorget

Triewaldsgränd

Benickebr.

Järntorget

Munkbroleden

Centralbron

Slussplan

Karl Johans Torg

Skeppsbron

Church

Railway

1. Riksbron
2. House of Parliament (Riksdagshuset)
3. Stallbron
4. Riddarhuset (House of Nobility)
5. Riddar House Square (Riddarhustorget)
6. Stampen
7. Gästorget
8. Stortorget
9. German Church (Tyska Kyrkan)
10. Prästgatan
11. An ice cream shop
12. Iron Market (Järntorget)
13. Statue of a gentleman in dark glasses
14. Free-standing house
15. Tyska Brunnsplan
16. Brända Tomtem
17. Själagårdsbodarna
18. House at no. 3
19. Köpmantorget
20. Palace Hill (Slottsbacken)
21. Stockholm Cathedral (Storkyrkan)
22. Royal Palace outer courtyard (Stoltzholm Slot)
23. Kanslihusannexet (Government Annex) courtyard
24. North Bridge (Norrbro)

To your left is the:

9. German Church (Tyska Kyrkan), with its 96-meter (315-ft.) copper-clad spire, a notable landmark on Gamla Stan. The carillon plays four times a day: "Now Thank We All Our God" at 8am and 4pm and "Praise to the Lord, the Almighty, the King of Creation" at noon and 8pm, which, according to one history book, have been at the "top of the Gamla Stan hit parade for centuries." The church is dedicated to St. Gertrude, a 7th-century abbess and the patron saint of travelers. The church's baroque altar is 10 meters (33 ft.) high; the unusual octagonal pulpit is made of ebony and marble. Though the church is part of the Church of Sweden, the Sunday service is held in German.

From Stortorget, retrace your steps along Kåkbrinken (downhill this time) to Västerlånggatan, pausing to explore:

10. **Prästgatan,** which followed the inside of the old city wall. Turn left onto this diminutive street lined with streetlamps and bicycles. To get a feel for what it's like, you need only walk in about two streetlamps' worth (if you're hooked, continue along it—rather than the more touristic Västerlånggattan—as far as Tyska Brinken and the church there).

If you choose to pick up Västerlånggattan from Kåkbrinken, turn left onto it. You'll pass mostly clothing stores and some jewelry shops.

REFUELING STOPS If you're hungry, you're in luck, because in the middle of this block of Västerlånggatan, you'll find **11. an ice cream shop,** on your left, and **Michelangelo** Italian restaurant, on your right—two different but equally delectable choices.

Continue along Västerlånggatan, which dead-ends into the:

12. **Iron Market (Järntorget),** the second-oldest square in Stockholm. An iron yard used to stand here, but it was relocated to Södermalm in 1662. At the far end of this square, you'll notice a:

13. **statue of a gentleman in dark glasses.** That's Carl Michael Bellman, 18th-century songwriter and musician, who worked here at the Bank of Sweden when he was 17. On your right, you'll find a market, convenient if you need to pick up a few groceries. On your left, at no. 81, is a shop called Islands, which sells woolens from all the Nordic countries, including gorgeous sweaters from Norway. No. 83 houses Sundberg's Cafe, which has been here for almost 200 years.

From the square, return to Västerlånggatan and walk only a few yards to link up with Mårten Trotzigs Gränd. Turn right and walk up the steps to cross Präsgatan and follow Tyska Stallplan to Svartmangatan. At this intersection, take a moment to admire the:

14. **free-standing house** across the street and to your right. It's easy to imagine Ibsen's Nora inside. Turn left onto Svartmangatan. Very soon, you'll come to:

15. **Tyska Brunnsplan,** with a neoclassical well that has been

here since 1787. From here, take the right-hand fork in the road, along Själagårdsgatan, and follow it as far as:

16. **Brända Tomtem,** with a single chestnut tree at its center. This is my favorite well-hidden spot in all Gamla Stan. Under one ivy-covered doorway, you'll discover a little shop called:

17. **Själagårdsbodarna,** no. 7–9. It's crammed full of treasures for children and adults alike—best described as the Swedish equivalent to Americana. While you're in this little square, spy into the window of the:

18. **house at no. 3** to admire the hand-painted 17th-century ceiling. Follow Själagårdsgatan to the bottom of the hill. To your right is:

19. **Köpmantorget,** with a towering bronze statue of St. George slaying the dragon. The most impressive view (and photo opportunity) of it is from the street below, Österlånggatan, which follows Gamla Stan's ancient and long-gone eastern wall.

From here, follow Köpmangatan to Trädgårdstvårgränd, a street much shorter than its name, and turn right onto it. You'll walk through a courtyard and an alleyway that opens onto:

20. **Palace Hill (Slottsbacken),** a large square anchored with an obelisk that stretches to a height of 33.5 meters (110 ft.). Placed here in 1799, the obelisk is a memorial to the burghers who had defended Stockholm during the war with Russia. To your left is the:

21. **Stockholm Cathedral (Storkyrkan),** dating from 1279 and the oldest existing building in Stockholm. The exterior is primarily from the 1700s; the interior, from the 1400s. Inside the cathedral is a powerful oak statue of St. George slaying the dragon (you saw a copy of it back at Köpmantorget). Here you'll also see the oldest known painting of Stockholm, believed to have been painted in 1535; it portrays a small cluster of dwellings on a speck of an island (the land under Gamla Stan has risen considerably over the centuries). Walk in front of the cathedral and into the curved walkway of the:

22. **Royal Palace (Stoltzholm Slot) outer courtyard.** On your left will be a statue of 26-year-old Lady Christina Gyllenstierna, who for a period led the opposition to the Kalmar Union king, King Christian II (she did not lose her head in the ensuing bloodbath but she did lose her freedom for a time). Pass the statue and the gift shop, then turn right onto Storkyrkobrinken. Continue down this street, passing some shops and the Lady Hamilton Hotel, and you'll link up once again with Västerlånggatan, at which you'll turn right. On your left is a doorway with a small tunnel behind it; in Alice in Wonderland–style, wander through it and you will emerge into the large, circular:

23. **Kanslihusannexet (Government Annex) courtyard** and

outdoor dining area for Chapeau Claque, a popular restaurant and disco (the entrance to it is around the corner, on Salvigränd). Go back to Västerlånggatan to complete the tour. After you've crossed the first bridge, take the steps to your right alongside the House of Parliament, then follow the diagonal pathway in front of the Parliament building to link up with the:

24. **North Bridge (Norrbro),** which will take you back to Sergels Torg or Kungsträdgården. If you look toward Norrmalm, you will see the Opera House on your right; if you look back toward Gamla Stan, the Medieval Museum and Royal Palace will be on your right. They are excellent choices should you choose to do some in-depth indoor sight-seeing to learn more about this historic area. If you visit the palace in summer, you might happen upon a free concert in progress or see the Changing of the Guard, which occurs daily at noon (1pm on Sunday).

WALKING TOUR 2 — Djurgården

Start: Djurgården Bridge.
Finish: Djurgården Bridge.
Time: 2 hours.
Best Time: Late afternoon, but if you plan to visit some of the island's fine museums come earlier and see them before your walk.

For many citizens of Stockholm, this is a favorite outing, often made after work and toward the end of the day, when the light is at its most dazzling. I think it's the world's prettiest walk within a city. Some of the waters around the island, those known as Isbaldbarret, attract the largest variety of aquatic birds in northern Europe. You might want to pack a picnic; the surroundings inspire one. Begin at the:

1. **Djurgården Bridge (Djurgårdsbron),** designed in the Beaux Arts style. From here you'll see one of the prettiest views of Stockholm, a life-size picture postcard. In summer you can rent a bike across the bridge on Djurgården (you might choose to bike this route—and expand it—instead of walking it).

   Rather than cross the bridge, as your feet are probably telling you to do, stay on the Östermalm side and pick up the path along the water's edge that begins in:

2. **Nobel Parken.** From here the directions are simple: Follow the path at your own pace all the way to a second:

3. **bridge,** which is known as Djurgårdsbrunnbron. Follow the path along the water's edge. If you pass by in summer, you'll

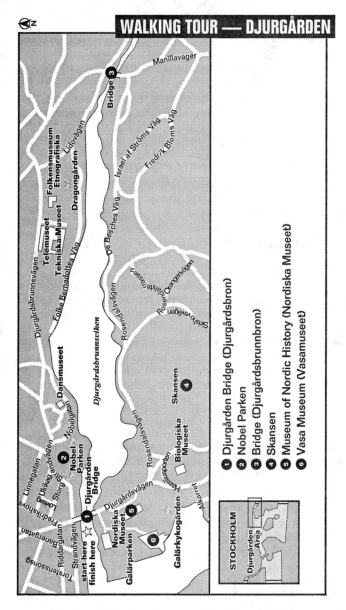

1 Djurgården Bridge (Djurgårdsbron)
2 Nobel Parken
3 Bridge (Djurgårdsbrunnbron)
4 Skansen
5 Museum of Nordic History (Nordiska Museet)
6 Vasa Museum (Vasamuseet)

STOCKHOLM

Djurgården Area

see sunbathers lolling by the water side. Cross the bridge onto
Djurgården and make the first right you can and follow the path
along the water's edge back to the first bridge to complete this
scenic and serene loop.

Just before you leave Djurgården, you'll see the entrance for:
4. Skansen, a century-old outdoor museum. This wooded area is

filled with authentic Swedish cottages and other buildings moved here from other parts of the country, and there's a small farmlike zoo—the only one in Stockholm—and a modern aquarium.

As you head back to the bridge you'll pass the:

5. **Museum of Nordic History (Nordiska Museet)** to your left. Inside the stately stone building are exhibits chronicling how Swedes have lived and labored over the past 500 years.

Beyond the museum, also on the left, is the:

6. **Vasa Museum (Vasamuseet),** built around an incredible, ornate warship called the *Vasa.* She sank on her maiden voyage out of Stockholm harbor in 1628, was delivered from her watery resting place in 1961, and has become the biggest tourist attraction in Stockholm.

REFUELING STOP If you're eager for something to eat or drink before heading back to Norrmalm, walk along Djurgardsvägen, the island's main road that passes the Vasa and Nordic museums, to **Cafe Blå Porten,** at Djurgårdensvägen 64. The cafe, in front of the Liljevalch Art Gallery, is not fancy, but you can get light fare such as soups and salads, served cafeteria-style.

After your stop, you may want to wander back to Norrmalm on foot, or pick up either bus no. 47 or bus no. 69; look for the bus-stop sign on the main thoroughfare near the Museum of Nordic History.

WALKING TOUR 3 — Skeppsholmen & Kastellholmen

Start: Skeppsholmen Bridge.
Finish: AF *Chapman.*
Time: 1 hour, not including breaks and visits to museums.
Best Time: Morning, so you can allow ample time for museumgoing afterward (there are three from which to choose).

Compared to Djurgården, the islands of Skeppsholmen and Kastellholmen are tiny; but they are lovely and so easy to explore on a short outing. Begin at the:

1. **Skeppsholmen Bridge,** right beside the National Museum and just below the landmark Grand Hotel. Cross the bridge onto Skeppsholmen, taking a moment en route to enjoy the tranquil views of Gamla Stan and the sleek tour boats that ply the waters

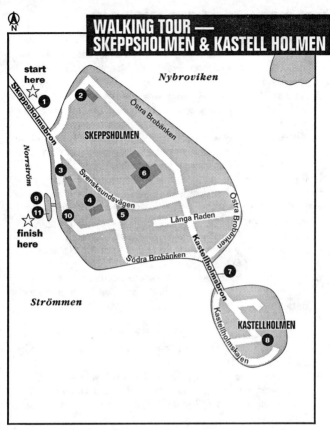

WALKING TOUR —
SKEPPSHOLMEN & KASTELL HOLMEN

around Stockholm. Directly in front of you is the AF *Chapman,* a three-masted schooner that has served as a youth hostel since 1949.

Cross the bridge onto the island. To your left, you'll see a long, amber-colored building. It's the:

2. Museum of Far Eastern Antiquities (Östasiatiska

Museet), with exhibits that include Chinese painting, sculpture, and ceramics; Indian sculpture; and Japanese and Korean art. There is a gift shop. Follow the main road, Svensksundsvägen; on the right, you'll pass the:

3. **Admiral's House (Admiraliteshuset),** a redbrick building with two small turrets, which now houses city offices. Also on your right is the:

4. **Architecture Museum (Arkitekturmuseet),** a small museum with changing exhibits and films, some in English. There are also archives and an architecture bookstore here. (The hill just above the museum, with a small brick building on it, is a secluded spot where you can sit and watch the world go by.) Back on the road, keep left when you get to the fork. On the right you'll see the:

5. **"Fantastic Paradise,"** the whimsical, colorful, and locally controversial sculpture by Niki de Saint Phalle with Jean Tinguely (1966) that is part of the:

6. **Museum of Modern Art (Moderna Museet),** on the other side of the road. The building also houses a small photography museum, as well as a cafe with outdoor seating in summer (keep it in mind for the end of the tour).

Continue along Svensksundsvägen until you can go no farther (unless you want to take a swim), and turn right onto Östra Brobänken. Follow it along the water's edge to the:

7. **Kastellholmen Bridge.** To your left you will see the Kaknäs TV Tower, the highest structure in Scandinavia, and the roller coaster of Gröna Lund (or Tivoli) amusement park. Cross the bridge onto:

8. **Kastellholmen,** a drop of an island that you can easily reconnoiter in 15 minutes. Once you've crossed the bridge, look back for a pleasant view of the Vasa Museum and the Museum of Nordic History on Djurgården. From here, follow the pathway leading uphill, keeping to the left and following the signs to Kastellet, a minicastle of sorts. (If you're not a good climber or don't like maneuvering through rocks, take the right fork.)

From the top of the hill, there's a nice view of the Viking Line dock (the ship provides regular ferry service between Stockholm and Helsinki). As you make your way down the hill to the south shore of Kastellholmen, you'll pass tidy houses and well-tended gardens.

Continue along the path to the water's edge; after you round the bend, the compact buildings of Gamla Stan and the spire of the German Church will come into view. The path will bring you back to the bridge and Skeppsholmen.

Turn left onto Södra Brobänken, which will lead you back to the "Fantastic Paradise" sculpture, on your right.

REFUELING STOP In the Museum of Modern Art, there is a nice little **cafe** where you can get hot or cold meals and ice cream. You'll enjoy the seating inside or out. Not surprisingly, the cafe attracts an arty crowd.

From the "Fantastic Paradise," hang a left and follow the low road, Vastra Brobänken (it's the one closest to the water) to the:

9. **AF *Chapman,*** a three-masted schooner that's now a youth hostel, not to mention a striking part of the Stockholm cityscape. If you've happened along during the hours it's open, climb aboard and visit the reception area. Here the staff keeps a notebook (called the *Stockholm Guide*) filled with listings of inexpensive restaurants and things to do that won't exceed your budget for entertainment.

Right across the street from the *Chapman* is its sister hostel the:

10. **STF Vandrarhem.** Both hostels have a public telephone inside, should you need one. Both are closed from noon to 3pm.

FINAL REFUELING STOP In summer, the AF *Chapman* runs a **11. cafe** above deck that is open to the public, not just to the hostelers on board. Besides serving inexpensive snacks and light meals, it offers a great view of Gamla Stan and the harbor. It's a relaxed atmosphere in which you'll meet other people, most of them travelers like you.

WALKING TOUR 4 —— Södermalm

Start: Södermalmstorg.
Finish: The Black & Brown Inn.
Time: 1 hour.
Best Time: Weekdays and Saturday mid-morning to early afternoon, when the shops are open.

With all the hubbub of Norrmalm and Gamla Stan, the quieter island of Södermalm often gets overlooked. That's unfortunate because with its share of shops, eateries, and nightlife, Södermalm's appeal is on a more local and less grand scale. This walking/shopping tour is short, encompassing just a few blocks of one street—and just one side of the street at that.

The cobblestoned street of Hornsgatan (often called the "Hump") is well loved by Stockholmers. It's filled mainly with small unique shops that will appeal even to nonshoppers. The shopowners are open and friendly, making this a "Meet the People" tour, if you will. And if you come away with a souvenir of Stockholm—some artwork, a ceramic candleholder, a wooden toy, some flashy earrings—more's the better.

Take the T-Bana to the Slussen stop and exit onto:

1. **Södermalmstorg,** a busy square where you're likely to find vendors with carts of flowers and fruits. As you face Gamla Stan to the north, you will see the:

2. **Stockholm City Museum (Stockholmstadsmuseet),** to the left. It portrays the city in centuries past in paintings, drawings, models, and sometimes photographs. There's a bookstore that usually has in stock *The Old Town* by Beatrice Glase and Gosta Glase, an excellent history of and guide to Gamla Stan.

   Back at Södermalmstorg, to the right you'll notice a large, vertical structure. That's the:

3. **Katarina Elevator,** whose only purpose is to lift people up seven stories for a sweeping view of the city and harbor or to save them the climb up the Södermalm cliffs behind the square (the cliffs provide equally lovely views). There's a small admission charge to get a lift from Katarina.

REFUELING STOPS   You may visit the small **cafe in the Stockholm City Museum,** which, appropriately, looks like a cafe might have looked 100 or so years ago. Located on Södermalmstorg in the squat blue building opposite the Stockholm City Museum is **Strömmen.** This glorified coffee shop has a view of Gamla Stan and the harbor that many fancy "four-fork" restaurants would fast for. Strömmen is a fun place for an economical breakfast, lunch, or early supper. If you want to push on with the tour rather than stop now for a cup of coffee or a snack, keep this place in mind for later.

From Södermalmstorg, walk to Hornsgatan by crossing the square in front of the Stockholm City Museum. You'll see the flags of the Scandic Crown Hotel, but you'll come to Hornsgatan before you come to the hotel (it's 1 block away from the hotel). Turn left and stay on the right-hand side of the street for the duration of the walk. You'll pass many unique, inviting shops and galleries. I've mentioned only some favorites here. The first place that will surely beckon you inside is:

4. **Blås & Knåda,** Hornsgatan 26 and Pustegränd, a pottery and ceramics gallery with an exquisite selection of work (all for sale). Just down the street, at:

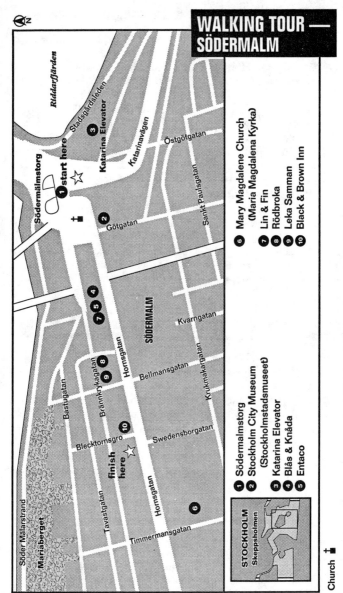

6 Mary Magdalene Church
(Maria Magdalena Kyrka)
7 Lin & Fin
8 Rödbroka
9 Leka Samman
10 Black & Brown Inn

1 Södermalmstorg
2 Stockholm City Museum
(Stockholmstadsmuseet)
3 Katarina Elevator
4 Blås & Knåda
5 Entaco

STOCKHOLM
Skeppsholmen

Church ✝

5. Entaco, Hornsgatan 32, Curt Johansson sells used cameras (if you collect them, be sure to look at his collection), as well as such essentials as film and batteries.

To your left you'll see the:

6. Mary Magdalene Church (Maria Magdalena Kyrka).
Continue strolling until you come to:

7. Lin & Fin, Hornsgatan 46, a Nordic treasure chest of handmade goods from Sweden, Norway, Denmark, and Finland. The prices are as attractive as the items for sale. Next door, at:

8. **Rödbroka,** Hornsgatan 48, you'll find locally designed and manufactured clothing, along with some toys and accessories for kids' rooms. Stroll a little farther, until you come to:

9. **Leka Samman,** Hornsgatan 50 A, where you'll assuredly be tempted to linger. Kerstin and Tomas Friberger have retired from other careers to run this compelling toy shop, where the emphasis is on items that encourage harmony, equality, and interactive play between parents and children.

FINAL REFUELING STOP The **10. Black & Brown Inn,** at Hornsgatan 50 B on the corner of Blecktornsgränd, is the area's landmark bar. It's Scottish, not Swedish, in character—from the plaid wallpaper to the kilts worn by the bartenders. The simple fare ranges from fish 'n' chips to burgers to Swedish hash. And, of course, there's plenty of international beers from which to choose.

WALKING TOUR 5 — Downtown

Start: Sweden House.
Finish: NK department store.
Time: 2 hours.
Best Time: Anytime but lunchtime, when the streets and cafes are jammed with 9-to-5ers on the loose. (If you plan to visit the Hallwyl Museum, be aware that during summer the English tour is given Tuesday through Sunday at 1pm; off-season it is given on Sunday only at 1pm. Tours of the Royal Dramatic Theater are given in summer daily at 3pm, so if that's of interest, you may want to time your tour accordingly.)

Begin the tour at:

1. **Sweden House,** Hamngatan 27, facing Kungsträdgården. If you need any maps, information, or even stamps, the Stockholm Information Service counter (inside Sweden House) is the place to go. From here, turn right onto Hamngatan and walk to the:

2. **Hallwyl Museum (Hallwylska Museet),** Hamngatan 4, the former home of Countess Wilhelmina von Hallwyl, filled with her eclectic collections of paintings, silver, porcelain, and weapons. From here, continue along Hamngatan until you get to Birger Jarlsgatan. Just around the corner is the office of:

3. **American Express,** Birger Jarlsgatan 1, a mecca for travelers where they can exchange money, pick up mail, and leave a

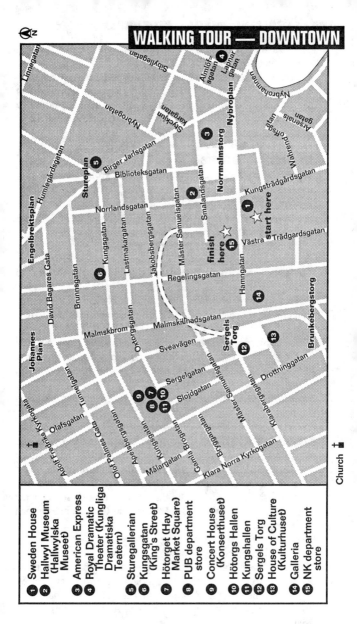

Sweden House
Hallwyl Museum (Hallwylska Museet)
American Express
Royal Dramatic Theater (Kungliga Dramatiska Teatern)
Sturegallerian
Kungsgatan (King's Street)
Hötorget (Hay Market Square)
PUB department store
Concert House (Konserthuset)
Hötorgs Hallen
Kungshallen
Sergels Torg
House of Culture (Kulturhuset)
Galleria
NK department store

forwarding address when they move on. This particular AmEx office is outstanding in its helpfulness. On Nybroplan, where Hamngatan meets Birger Jarlsgatan, you'll find the:

4. Royal Dramatic Theater (Kungliga Dramatiska Teatern). The current structure dates from 1907, but the theater itself was founded by King Gustav III in 1787. One of

Europe's finest playhouses, it has four different stages. (As noted above, the tour is given at 3pm daily.)

Follow Birger Jarlsgatan to Stureplan and:

5. Sturegallerian, a new trendy shopping complex with an 18th-century facade and modern interior. This mall houses a good bookstore, Hedengrens Bokhandel (check out the travel and fiction sections downstairs).

REFUELING STOPS In Sturegallerian, you'll find several **cafes** and an **ice cream counter** (on the ground-floor level in the back) that sells delicious sorbets. **Arnold's,** at Birger Jarlsgatan 20, has a whimsical decor, a varied menu, and good prices on beer. Grab a window seat overlooking the bustling activity of Stureplan.

From Stureplan, pick up:

6. Kungsgatan (King's Street). This wide, busy street leads to Sveavägen and:

7. Hötorget (Hay Market Square), a lively gathering spot for fruit and flower vendors and their customers. Facing the square is the:

8. PUB department store, where Greta Gustafsson worked before moving to the United States and becoming the legendary film actress Garbo. On the south side of Hötorget, on Sveavägen, is Stockholm's:

9. Concert House (Konserthuset), where symphony concerts are held.

REFUELING STOPS Hötorget must have been planned with the eat-and-run crowd in mind. There's the outdoor market itself. Add to that **10. Hötorgs Hallen,** on the south side of the square (take the escalator down), where you can sample fast food from around the world or pick up some picnic supplies. Across Hötorget is **11. Kungshallen,** an indoor mall with many more fast-food stands.

From Hötorget, head south on Sveavägen to:

12. Sergels Torg and its distinctive obelisk sculpture. This is the pulsing heart of commercial Stockholm. Here you'll find the SL Center on the lower level, where you can obtain information on local transportation, maps, and tickets. Also at Sergels Torg is the:

13. House of Culture (Kulturhuset), Sergels Torg 3, a local gathering place day and night. You can do everything here from listening to records on headsets to visiting art galleries to attending concerts. (There's often a free, impromptu musical performance going on outside as well.)

Pick up Hamngatan here and follow it east to:

14. Gallerian, Hamngatan 37, a mall with fast-food eateries and shops. Galleriet, located in the back, sells the cheapest postcards in town. The T-Centralen subway stop is here.

Continue along Hamngatan to the:

15. NK department store, Hamngatan 18-20, the city's most exclusive place to shop. The merchandise is of top quality, with prices to match. International newspapers and magazines are sold in its Service Center.

FINAL REFUELING STOP   **NK** boasts several eateries: on the fourth floor, there's a pretty little restaurant called **Plates** and right beside it is a pleasant **cafeteria.** A **coffee shop** popular with students can be found in the sub-basement (prices are lowest here).

CHAPTER 8

STOCKHOLM SHOPPING

1. THE SHOPPING SCENE
2. SHOPPING A TO Z

You'll never hear about people picking up and flying to Sweden for a shopping excursion—certainly not to pick up a Volvo or a Saab. Merchandise here is expensive, and if what you've got a hankering to buy is not out of the ordinary, you can probably get it at home for less money. On the positive side, Swedish stores usually stock items of the highest quality, and what you do buy should outlast you.

1. THE SHOPPING SCENE

Store Hours In general, shops are open Monday through Friday from 9:30am to 6pm, and on Saturday from 10am to 2pm. Department stores are open later.

TAXES & REFUNDS

Tax-Free Shopping Cheques The tax on goods in Sweden is 25%. But many stores offer tax rebates to tourists spending 100 Kr ($18.20) or more. Here's how to get your refund: First you must buy from a participating shop, look for a blue-and-yellow sticker in the window. When you make your purchase, ask the retailer for a Tax-Free Shopping Cheque, which is valid for 1 month. Keep your purchase sealed until you leave the country. At any border crossing, whether you leave by car, plane, or ferry, show both the check (to which you must add your name, address, and passport number) and the *sealed* purchase to an official at the tax-free offices. You will receive a cash refund—of 14% to 18% of the tax paid on the purchase—in U.S. dollars (or seven other currencies), minus a small service charge. At the airport, remember not to check your luggage containing the purchase until you have received your refund.

BEST BUYS

Favorite purchases include crystal (particularly Orrefors and Kosta Boda, which is produced in Småland in southern Sweden), clothing, and Scandinavian-design furniture. Take a good look at some of the high-tech designs that have made Sweden famous. This is a land of inventors, after all, and they have given us the refrigerator, vaccuum cleaner, and a dream of a camera called Hasselblad, to name but a few.

I'm a dyed-in-the-wool budget traveler, but I do give in to the occasional splurge. On my first trip to Stockholm a number of years ago, I bought a striking wool scarf at the NK department store (I had seen so many stylish Swedish women wearing them during my visit). The purchase was $50 and I would never have made it at home; but the scarf is a lovely reminder of a lovely city, and years later I still wear it frequently and get compliments on it.

For my next Swedish splurge, I'm planning to buy a brandy decanter so that I can claim some of the country's exquisitely crafted crystal for my own.

For those visits when I just can't afford to shop, I happily make do with postcards, museum prints, and tape cassettes. But that doesn't keep me out of the upscale shops; I love to look and make mental notes about what I'll be able to afford next time. And it doesn't cost anything to admire the craftsmanship that has made Sweden world-famous in design.

SHOPPING AREAS

For the best shopping and window shopping in Stockholm, stroll along the quiet streets of Gamla Stan, particularly its main thoroughfare, **Västerlånggatan,** which is filled with boutiques, art galleries, and jewelry stores. Fewer, though similarly winsome, shops may be found along **Hornsgatan** on Södermalm. In Norrmalm, streets that prompt browsing include **Hamngatan** (with the NK department store and Gallerian shopping center), **Birger Jarlsgatan** (with Sturegallerian shopping center), and **Biblioteksgatan.**

Along the pedestrian street of Drottninggatan—leading through Norrmalm from Hötorget Square past the House of Culture into Gamla Stan—the stores aren't as tempting or upscale as those you'll find elsewhere. The street entertainers that show up here are good, though.

2. SHOPPING A TO Z

AUCTION

AUKTIONSVERKET (Auction Chambers), Jakobsgatan 10, Gallerian shopping mall. Tel. 14-24-40.

Visitors are welcome to bid or watch. Viewings are usually held on Wednesday and Saturday, but call to double-check times for

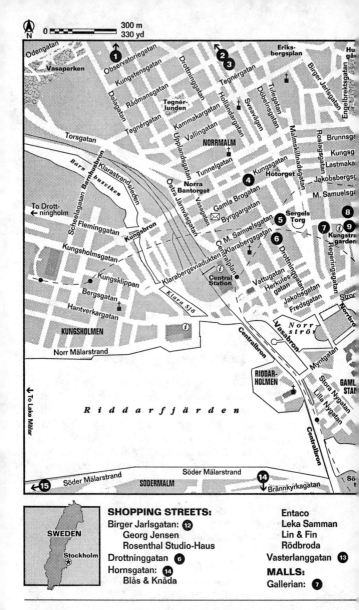

SHOPPING STREETS:

Birger Jarlsgatan: ⑫
  Georg Jensen
  Rosenthal Studio-Haus

Drottninggatan ⑥

Hornsgatan: ⑭
  Blås & Knåda

Entaco
Leka Samman
Lin & Fin
Rödbroda
Vasterlanggatan ⑬

MALLS:
Gallerian: ⑦

SWEDEN

Stockholm ✪

viewing and the auction itself. Be sure to ask what's up for bids on the day you want to visit.

BOOKSTORES

AKADEMI BOKHANDELN, Regeringsgatan and **Mäster Samuelsgatan.** Tel. 21-15-90.

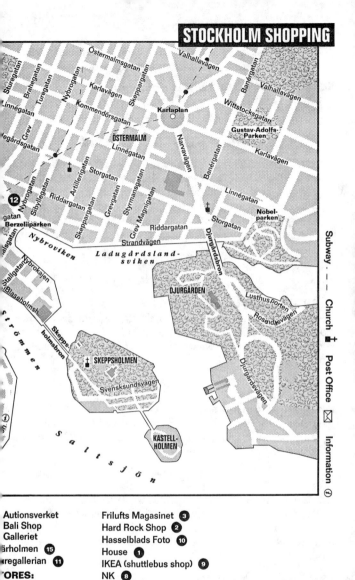

STOCKHOLM SHOPPING

Subway ‧ - - Church ✝ Post Office ⊠ Information ⊖

Autionsverket
Bali Shop
Galleriet
ärholmen **15**
uregallerian **11**
'ORES:
éns **5**

Frilufts Magasinet **3**
Hard Rock Shop **2**
Hasselblads Foto **10**
House **1**
IKEA (shuttlebus shop) **9**
NK **8**
PUB **4**

The best prices and a large selection are found here. Check out the bargain bin. Fiction is in the back on the left. Open: Monday through Friday from 9:30am to 6pm, and on Saturday from 10am to 2pm (3pm in winter).

HEDENGRENS BOKHANDEL, Stureplan **4** **in** **Sturegallerian. Tel. 08/611-5132.**

This large and impressive store has big travel and fiction sections downstairs. You'll also find a nice architecture section.

HEDENGRENS BOKHANDEL, Kungsgatan 4.

This is a small outpost of the large bookstore listed above. Here you'll find English language books at discounted prices.

CAMPING/OUTDOOR GEAR

FRILUFTS MAGASINET, Sveavägen 73 at Odengatan. Tel. 34-20-00. Also Hantverkargatan 38-40. Tel. 52-50-92.

⭐ If you need camping or outdoor gear, this store has a wide assortment. You'll find everything from cooking equipment to flashlights and batteries to raingear and Norwegian ski sweaters. The Sveavägen store is across the street from the Hard Rock Cafe.

CLOTHING

CHILDREN'S

RÖDBROKA, Hornsgatan 48. Tel. 42-16-89.

The kiddie clothes here are exclusively designed and made for this shop, where the prices are equivalent to those in the United States. Rödbroka also carries some toys and accessories for children's rooms.

WOMEN'S

LIN & FIN, Hornsgatan 46, Slussen. Tel. 702-15-92.

⭐ This shop has a limited but special selection of clothing in striking styles and colors, along with some jewelry. It also sells gifts and crafts (see below).

CRAFTS

LIN & FIN, Hornsgatan 46, Slussen. Tel. 702-15-92.

This shop carries colorful, carefully chosen handmade items from the Scandinavian countries and Finland. Reasonably priced, these crafts make great gifts and souvenirs. Most are small and easily packable.

BALI SHOP, Gallerian mall. Tel. 10-00-58.

This small shop, tucked in the back of the Gallerian on the street level, sells painted wood flowers, fruit, and animals from Bali. It's appealing in a non-Scandinavian way.

CRYSTAL

Check the crystal sections of the city's major department stores. You may find a sale.

ROSENTHAL STUDIO-HAUS, Birger Jarlsgatan 6. Tel. 21-66-01.

Not only do they have beautifully displayed crystal, pottery, and housewares, but they'll ship any item for you and deduct the VAT when they do so.

DEPARTMENT STORES

NK, Hamngatan 18-20. Tel. 762-80-00.

The Harrods of Stockholm, NK stands for Nordiska Kompaniet. Here you'll find beautifully displayed quality merchandise—clothing, household items, crystal, and much more—often at high prices. International newspapers and magazines are sold in the Service Center area. NK is conveniently located across the street from Sweden House.

PUB, Hötorget Square. Tel. 791-60-00.

Surely, Greta Garbo was PUB's most famous employee. If you don't believe it, visit the fifth floor of its Hötorgshuset building to see a small exhibit (conveniently located next to the coffee shop) on the young, then-unglamorous Greta, who caught the storeowner's eye and then modeled hats, gloves, and dresses for newspaper ads. Besides that, PUB has a great location overlooking the open-air market at Hötorget. An unusual plus for foreign travelers, the store accepts payment in foreign currency at any cash register.

FLEA MARKET

SKÄRHOLMEN SHOPPING CENTER, Skärholmen. Tel. 710-00-60.

This is northern Europe's largest flea market, with everything from junk to real treasures. Take the T-Bana line 13 to Skärholmen, about a 20-minute ride from Central Station. The shopping mall is on the left side of the town's main square. Follow the yellow sign that reads "Loppmarknaden." The market bustles all week long, but the weekends are the liveliest. It's open Monday through Friday from 11am to 6pm, on Saturday from 9am to 3pm. Admission on weekends is 6 Kr ($1.10) for adults, free for children; it's free to all on weekdays.

GIFTS

HARD ROCK SHOP, Sveavägen 75. Tel. 16-03-50.

No surprises here, just more of the fun, upbeat Hard Rock Cafe memorabilia that's quickly spreading from continent to continent.

HOME FURNISHINGS

HOUSE, Odengatan 79-81. Tel. 34-05-03.

⭐ If you're smitten with Scandinavian design—the clean lines and generous use of wood—head to House, where two floors display furniture and household items, many of museum quality, from Denmark, Finland, and Europe. Much of it is art deco–inspired, and most of the furniture is made of pine and birch. You can find small items, such as lamps, sconces, plates, vases, and picture frames. The store is located opposite Gustav Vasa Church, a block from the Odenplan subway stop.

IKEA, Kungens Kurva. Tel. 744-83-00.

If Scandinavian-design furniture, lamps, glassware, ceramics, and other household objects intrigue you, don't miss this store, which claims to be the largest home-furnishings store in the world. Located 25 minutes from the city center, it is served by a free special bus, which leaves from the front of Sweden House hourly, Monday through Friday only, from 11am to 5pm (returning hourly on the half hour).

JEWELRY

GEORG JENSEN, Birger Jarlsgatan 13. Tel. 20-59-22.

Jensen's trademark fine silver jewelry is found here, along with porcelain and glass from Royal Copenhagen.

MALLS

Downtown Stockholm has two shopping complexes that are as different as the Nordic summer and winter. The centrally located **Gallerian,** Hamngatan 37, is close to Sweden House and not unlike the generic malls at home, but you may find it of particular interest for the cheap postcards you can get there. The T-Centralen subway stop is here, as well. Its trendy counterpart, **Sturegallerian,** Stureplan 4 and Birger Jarlsgatan, has 50 upscale shops and has won awards for its design. Although the facade remains strictly 18th century, everything behind it is a modern amalgam of chrome, glass, and marble.

PHOTOGRAPHIC SUPPLIES

Film can be purchased and processed in shops on almost every street in the city center, especially in the major tourist areas. During the summer, some department stores offer two-for-the-price-of-one specials on film.

ENTACO, Hornsgatan 32, Slussen. Tel. 41-44-44.

Curt Johannsson sells used cameras, including some collector's models. Of course, if you need more basic items, like film and batteries, you can find them, too, in his little shop on Södermalm.

HASSELBLADS FOTO, Hamngatan 16. Tel. 21-40-42.

This fairly large store, right across from Sweden House, stocks most any camera supplies you might need, and it's a good place to come should you need a repair.

POSTCARDS

GALLERIET, Gallerian mall. Tel. 21-45-30.

Look for the large selection of sale postcards and notecards outside the shop. They have the best prices in Stockholm, about 1 Kr (20¢) a card. (If you buy notecards, ask for envelopes when you pay inside.)

POTTERY

BLÅS & KNÅDA, Hornsgatan 26. Tel. 42-77-67.

The selection is exquisite, so definitely come to look, even if you can't afford to buy—or limit your purchases to cups, vases, and candleholders.

TOYS

LEKA SAMMAN, Hornsgatan 50A. Tel. 714-96-00.

The name Leka Samman means "Play Together." Lovingly stocked and tended by Tomas and Kerstin Friberger, this shop features toys, dolls, games, musical instruments, and costumes from around the world. You'll even find cowboys and Indians interspersed with knights on horseback. The items, of natural materials, are designed to promote peace and equality, according to Mr. Friberger, who once taught urban design at Berkeley. The Friberger family is depicted in the quilt hanging inside the shop.

STOCKHOLM NIGHTS

On the late-night front, all is well in Stockholm. The nightlife in what was once a fairly staid capital city has undergone a major transformation over the last decade. Today, late-nighters mix and mingle in a thriving café scene, listen to live jazz, rock, and blues whenever they get the notion, and dance into the wee hours—usually at Kungsträdgården or on Gamla Stan or Södermalm.

For up-to-date information, check at the Stockholm Information Service, in *Stockholm This Week,* and in local newspapers (especially *Dagens Nyheter* from Thursday through Sunday) for details on upcoming events, some of which are announced in English on the Stockholm Information Service's "Events of the Day" recording (tel. 22-18-40). Students and seniors get special discounts at the major performance halls.

1. THE PERFORMING ARTS

In Stockholm the arts—opera, theater, and music—are well supported with state funds. This results in high-quality serious entertainment that is refreshingly affordable; public funding allows theaters to experiment with new, sometimes controversial ideas. Unfortunately for travelers coming to Stockholm during the summer, the Concert House and the Royal Opera House close for much of June, July, and August; the Royal Dramatic Theater takes a couple of weeks off, too.

CLASSICAL CONCERTS, OPERA, THEATER, & BALLET

CONCERT HOUSE (Konserthuset), Hötorget 8. Tel. 10-21-10.

MAJOR CONCERT & PERFORMANCE HALL BOX OFFICES

Concert House (Filharmonikerna i Konserthuset),
Hötorget 8. Tel. 10-21-10.
Globen, Johanneshov. Tel. 600-34-00.
Regina Theater, Drottninggatan 71A. Tel. 20-70-00.
Royal Dramatic Theater (Kungliga Dramatiska Teatern), Nybroplan at Birger Jarlsgatan. Tel. 667-06-80.
Royal Opera House (Kungliga Operan), Gustav Adolfs Torg. Tel. 24-82-40.

This hall is home to the Stockholm Philharmonic Orchestra, and performances are usually given on Wednesday, Thursday, and Saturday throughout the season—August through May. Touring companies sometimes light up the stage on other days throughout the year.

Prices: Tickets 48–150 Kr ($8.70–$27.30); students and seniors get 20% discount.

Open: Box office, Mon–Fri 10am–6pm, Sat 10am–1pm. **Closed:** June–July. **T-Bana:** Hötorget.

ROYAL DRAMATIC THEATER (Kungliga Dramatiska Teatern), Nybroplan at Birger Jarlsgatan. Tel. 667-06-80.

This is one of the great playhouses of Europe. The works performed here are almost exclusively in Swedish, but that shouldn't deter you. Occasionally, the stage is graced with ballet performances.

Tours: Summer, daily 3pm; rest of the year, Sat (only) 5:30pm.

Prices: 70–125 Kr ($12.70–$22.70) for large stage, 110–125 Kr ($20–$22.70) for small stage; anyone younger than 20 pays half price; students and seniors get 10% discount.

Open: Box office, Mon 10am–6pm, Tues–Sat 10am–7pm, Sun noon–4pm. **Closed:** 2 weeks in summer. T-Bana: Kungsträdgården.

ROYAL OPERA HOUSE (Kungliga Operan), Gustav Adolfs Torg. Tel. 24-82-40.

The Kungliga Operan, now beautifully restored, is home to the Swedish Royal Opera. There is an emphasis on popular works like *Don Giovanni, Madame Butterfly,* and *Carmen*—translated into Swedish. The season runs from December to the beginning of June. Call or visit the box office for a current schedule.

Prices: Tickets 110–200 Kr ($20–$36.35); students can buy most tickets at discount of almost 50%.

Open: Box office, Mon–Fri 11am–7:30pm (to 6pm when no performance is scheduled), Sat 11am–3pm (later on performance days). Tickets are sold up to month in advance. **Closed:** Mid-June–mid-Aug.

REGINA THEATER, Drottninggatan 71A. Tel. 20-70-00.

   Mounting productions since 1981, the Regina is Sweden's only English-language theater and the only equity theater in Europe besides Vienna's English Theater—this doesn't ensure consistently stellar performances, however. Seating for 300 people is open and all seats are good. Half a dozen or more productions are given each year. The theater has its own pub, a congenial place to meet for a beer or snack before the 7:30 curtain.

   Prices: 125 Kr ($22.70). Students get 25% discount.
   Open: Box office, Mon noon–6pm, Tues–Sun noon–7:30pm.
Closed: Mon and June–Aug. **T-Bana:** Hötorget.

---

2. THE CLUB & MUSIC SCENE

JAZZ, BLUES & ROCK

STAMPEN, Stora Nygatan 5, in Gamla Stan. Tel. 20-57-93.

   ⭐ Stampen, Stockholm's lively center for jazz, has been around since 1967. Two bands perform here nightly. From the ceiling above the upstairs stage hangs a cello, a Confederate flag, a wooden sleigh, an artificial limb—all vestiges from the days when this was a pawnshop. The second stage is in the more subdued downstairs room. Minimum age is 23. Like most of the city's other live music clubs, Stampen is located in Gamla Stan.

   Admission: Mon 60 Kr ($10.90), Tues after 8pm 70 Kr ($12.70), Wed–Thurs 80 Kr ($14.55), Fri–Sat 100 Kr ($18.20), more if it's a big band. Free Tues 5–8pm and Sat 1–5pm.

   Open: Mon 8pm–midnight, Tues–Fri 8pm–1am, Sat–Sun 1–5pm and 8pm–1am. **Closed:** Sun in winter. **T–Bana:** Gamla Stan.

ENGELEN, Kornhamnstorg 59B, in Gamla Stan. Tel. 10-07-22.

   Engelen (the name means "Angel") provides a stage for local bands nightly. Live music is performed upstairs from 8:30pm until midnight, while a DJ spins dance music downstairs until 3am. The mid-20s crowd arrives early, before 10pm, especially on weekends, when the place is packed. Patrons are welcome to join in an open jam on Sunday from 5:30 to 8:30pm. Hungry? Try the all-you-can-eat smorgasbord.

Admission: Mon–Tues 30 Kr ($5.45), Wed–Thurs and Sun 35 Kr ($6.35), Fri–Sat 50–60 Kr ($9.10–$10.90).

Prices: Smorgasbord 84 Kr ($15.30); half liter of beer 40 Kr ($7.30); bottle of house wine 95 Kr ($17.30).

Open: Daily 5pm–3am. **T-Bana:** Gamla Stan.

KAOS, Stora Nygatan 21, in Gamla Stan. Tel. 20-58-86.

This is an informal bilevel cafe and club with frequent live music. Several nights a week an additional stage is opened downstairs, where a second band performs. Sunday is dedicated to the blues.

Admission: Sun–Thurs 30 Kr ($5.45) after 7:30pm, Fri–Sat 45 Kr ($8.20).

Open: Mon–Fri 11am–1am, Sat–Sun 6pm–1am. **T-Bana:** Gamla Stan.

MOSEBACKE ESTABLISSEMENT, Mosebacke Torg 1-3, in Södermalm. Tel. 41-90-20.

The cabaret performed at Mosebacke attracts an older crowd, while people of all ages come in droves to listen to local rock, blues, and jazz bands. The big plus for budgeteers is the free outdoor entertainment in summer from 8pm to 11pm nightly. Call for the schedule of upcoming entertainment.

Admission: 30–120 Kr ($5.45–$21.80), depending on band; free outdoors in summer.

Open: Daily 5pm–midnight. **T-Bana:** Slussen.

ROCK/POP CONCERTS

GLOBEN, Johanneshov. Tel. 600-34-00.

An unmistakably round, white presence in the Stockholm cityscape, the Globe is the place to come for big rock concerts, to see and hear international pop music stars—Billy Joel, Cher, and Janet Jackson have performed here in the past couple of years. Tickets vary according to concert, so call for upcoming shows, schedules, and prices.

T-Bana: Globen.

DANCE CLUBS/DISCOS

If starting late means it's good, then Stockholm's dance clubs are outstanding. Most are open for dinner, then there's a lull for a few hours before the diehards arrive around midnight. Long lines outside tend to indicate the latest happening spot.

CAFE OPERA, Kungsträdgården, behind Royal Opera House. Tel. 11-00-26.

This is certainly one of the most exclusive places in town—one of those upscale spots you read about in the society pages—and it looks so appealing when you gaze through the windows. Although the line to get in can be long, the door policy is not as selective as at similar clubs in other cities (perhaps that's why there's human gridlock inside). Some folks have the expensive dinners here. But the real socializing doesn't start until after midnight. Drinks are—as you would expect—expensive. If you prefer to escape the frenzy (if only momentarily), turn right at the entrance instead of left to Cafe Opera, pass through the Opera Bar (where artists and journalists strike poses), and make your way to the congenial Bakfickan, or Back Pocket Bar (see "The Bar Scene," below).

Admission: Free before midnight, 60 Kr ($10.90) midnight–2am.

Prices: Half liter of beer 51 Kr ($9.30).

Open: Mon–Sat 11:30am–3am, Sun 1pm–3am. **T-Bana:** Kungsträdgården.

DAILY NEWS CAFE, Kungsträdgården. Tel. 21-56-55.

Just doors away from Cafe Opera is another "in" spot with an exclusive door policy, the Daily News Cafe. With an elaborate light show and good sound, it's more dance-oriented than the Opera. The crowd customarily arrives late. The dance floor is small, as is the Backstage bar downstairs. TV monitors provide play-by-play action of the events taking place next door at Melody.

Admission: Sun–Thurs 50 Kr ($9.10), Fri–Sat 60 Kr ($10.90); when there's a live band, 80–100 Kr ($16.20–$18.20).

Open: Daily 11:30am–3am; DJ 9pm–3am. **T-Bana:** Kungsträdgården.

MELODY, Kungsträdgården. Tel. 10-03-40.

It moved next door to the Daily News Cafe in 1990 from a theater it used to call home, but brought the large dance floor and posters with it. Inside, you'll find a stage and a busy bar; a balcony overlooks the dance floor. The crowd is mixed; minimum age, 23. Expect long lines on weekends.

Admission: 50 Kr ($9.10); 80–115 Kr ($14.55–$20.90) for concerts.

Open: Daily 7pm–3am. **T-Bana:** Kungsträdgården.

GÖTA KÄLLARE, in Medborgarplatsen subway stop, in Södermalm. Tel. 42-08-28.

Well-dressed older couples with a penchant for dancing cheek-to-cheek congregate here to enjoy the live bands, large dance floors, Platters-style music, and each other. Live bands alternate with disco music; the minimum age is 25.

Admission: 70 Kr ($12.70).

Open: Mon–Sat 8pm–2:30am. It's a good idea to call and check times. **T-Bana:** Medborgarplatsen.

GAY DISCO

PRIDE, Sveavägen 57. Tel. 736-0-12.
This small disco is in the back of the gay center, RFSL-Huset, which also houses Alice B., a popular restaurant and a good spot to dine before dancing. Look for the green-and-pink neon sign that says "Pride."
Admission: Sat only 60 Kr ($10.90).
Open: Nightly 9pm–1am. First Fri of month is lesbian night, but men are still welcome at bar. **T-Bana:** Rådmansgatan. **Bus:** 52.

3. THE BAR SCENE

Because of the astronomical price of alcohol, which is heavily taxed, most customers nurse their drinks for a long time, and understanding waiters don't hurry them. For budget travelers, even a short dip in a local watering hole (and there are many inviting ones) is a splurge. With that in mind, here are some favorites.

WESTERMANNS BAR, Tyska Brinken 30, in Gamla Stan. Tel. 10-12-40.
Bypass the restaurant and go upstairs to this honky-tonk bar that boasts the best-preserved wooden ceiling in Stockholm, dating from 1648. Once or twice a month, a live band performs. The entrance is on Stora Nygatan.
Prices: Beer from 5–9pm, 28 Kr ($5.10); afterward, 35 Kr ($6.35); glass of wine 33 Kr ($6).
Open: Daily from 5pm–midnight (they sometimes close on Sun in winter). **T-Bana:** Gamla Stan.

BAKFICKAN, Operahuset, Kungsträdgården. Tel. 20-77-45.
The name Bakfickan means "Back Pocket Bar"; this place is as tiny as its name implies, not to mention one of Stockholm's best-kept secrets—from out-of-towners who aren't Frommer guide readers, anyway. Patrons sit around the bar (where service is

IMPRESSIONS

Girls very pretty and not disfigured by paint and hairdressing. All look sexually and socially satisfied.
—EVELYN WAUGH
(*DIARY*, AUGUST 18, 1947)

quickest) or at bar stools along the tiled walls. The quietest time is from 2 to 5pm. Good food is available all day.

Prices: Daily food specials 49–82 Kr ($8.90–$14.90); daily salad 49 Kr ($8.90); beer 47 Kr ($8.55); glass of wine 43 Kr ($7.80).

Open: Mon–Sat 11:30am–11:30pm. **T-Bana:** Kungsträd-gården.

TENNSTOPET, Dalagatan 50, at Odenplan. Tel. 32-25-18.

⭐ You'll have to fight local artists and journalists for a seat at the bar here at Stockholm's oldest pub. With a bright-red awning outside and equally red decor inside, Tennstopet is quite distinctive. There's a dart room in back and a couple of cozy tables in between it and the crowded bar area. A restaurant on the premises serves traditional Swedish fare in a pretty setting, but the prices exceed budget range. (Don't let that stop you from taking a look at the beautiful ceiling, though.)

Prices: Bass Pale Ale, McEwan's Export, Guinness Stout, and other imports—39 Kr ($7.10).

Open: Mon–Fri 11:30am–12:30am, Sat 2pm–1am, Sun 4pm–12:30am. **T-Bana:** Odenplan.

BLACK & BROWN INN, Hornsgatan 50 B, in Södermalm. Tel. 44-82-80.

The bartenders are decked out in kilts in this landmark tavern with booths, windowseats, and plaid wallpaper. Scottish and Irish music plays constantly, and fish 'n' chips, burgers and *pytt i panna* (Swedish hash) complement the beers.

Prices: Bottle of beer 37 Kr ($6.70); international beers 41 Kr ($7.45).

Open: Mon–Fri 4pm–midnight; Sat–Sun 7pm–midnight. **T-Bana:** Mariatorget.

---

4. MORE ENTERTAINMENT

SUMMER FARE

Free open-air park performances by the **Parkteatern (Parks Theater)** begin in June and continue throughout the summer; **Sommarnättskonserter (Summer Night Concerts),** on the main staircase of the National Museum, start in July and run through the end of August; and **folk dancing at Skansen** occurs nightly at 7pm. Skansen also hosts concerts and dancing. For more information, check with the Stockholm Information Service.

In the summer, **jazz cruises** (aboard the S/S Björksjärden, tel. 23-33-75) provide an exhilarating way to experience Stockholm on the water while enjoying upbeat entertainment under the stars. This is a good way to meet Swedish people, who enjoy this sort of outing as much as tourists do. The boats usually stop at an island so revelers can dance on shore.

CHURCH CONCERTS

Many of the city's churches—the **Stockholm Cathedral,** on Gamla Stan; **Jacob's Church,** near the Royal Opera House; and **Hedvig Eleonora,** in Östermalm, for instance—often host free evening and afternoon concerts year round. Check listings under "Music" in *Stockholm This Week* or look for announcements posted in front of individual churches.

MOVIES

Tickets for most films, including American blockbusters and other international hits, generally cost 60 Kr ($10.90). Foreign films are usually screened in their original language with Swedish subtitles. **Röda Kvarn,** Biblioteksgatan 5 (tel. 84-05-00 from 12:30 to 9pm), is a pleasant, centrally located cinema that usually offers one mid-afternoon and two evening shows.

CHAPTER 10

EASY EXCURSIONS FROM STOCKHOLM

1. DROTTNINGHOLM
2. MARIEFRED
3. VAXHOLM
4. ARCHIPELAGO
   EXPLORATION

Stockholm is the "City on the Water," and nearby places of interest are, as you would expect, all accessible by boat. This makes getting there just as invigorating as actually arriving and exploring.

1. DROTTNINGHOLM

The palace of the present-day Swedish King, Carl XVI Gustaf, and Queen Silvia is open to visitors year round. The 17th-century rococo structure is just 7 miles from the city center. In addition to the State Apartments, the Drottningholm grounds encompass a theater dating from 1766 and an exotic Chinese Pavilion.

GETTING THERE

There are three ways of reaching Drottningholm. The first, and most exciting, is by steamboat via Lake Mälaren; the trip takes 50 minutes and costs 50 Kr ($9.10) one way, 70 Kr ($12.70) round trip (half price for children). Boats leave from Stadshusbron, opposite Stockholm's City Hall, on the hour from 10am to 2pm (to 4pm on weekends) daily from late April to early June, and from 10am to 4pm and at 6pm daily from early June to mid-August. Call **Strömma Kanalbolaget** at 23-33-75 for more information and for autumn sailings.

Stockholm Sightseeing offers trips to Drottningholm in turn-of-the-century boats for 30 Kr ($5.45) one way, 60 Kr ($10.10) round trip. Boats depart every hour from 9:30am to 4:30pm from early May to early June, and from 9:30am to 6:30pm from early June to mid-August. Call 24-04-70 for more information.

You may also take the **T-Bana** to Brommaplan and then connect to any Mälarö bus for Drottningholm.

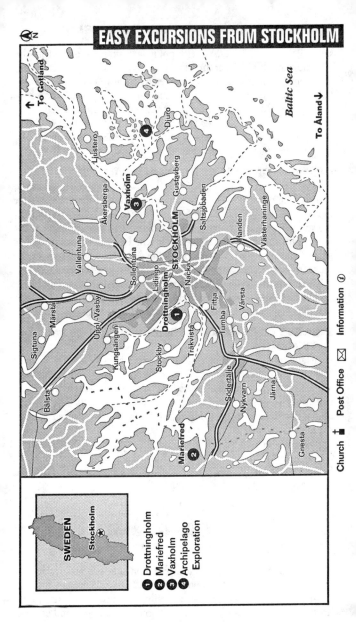

Church ┿   Post Office ⊠   Information ⓘ

SWEDEN
Stockholm ✪

1 Drottningholm
2 Mariefred
3 Vaxholm
4 Archipelago Exploration

WHAT TO SEE & DO

DROTTNINGHOLM PALACE (Drottningholm Slott). Tel. 759-03-10.

Built for Sweden's Queen Eleonora in 1662, this four-story palace with two-story wings has often been referred to as a "little Versailles." The interior dazzles with opulent furniture and art from the 17th through the 19th century, including painted ceilings, ornate gold chandeliers, Chinese vases, and other luxurious details. Vast sculptured gardens surround the palace, and from time to time visitors may even spot the down-to-earth royal couple taking a stroll.

Admission: 25 Kr ($4.55) for adults, 20 Kr ($3.65) for children.

Open: May–Aug, daily 11am–4:30pm; Sept, Mon–Fri 1–3:30pm, Sat–Sun noon–3:30pm. **Closed:** Oct–Apr.

DROTTNINGHOLM COURT THEATER. Tel. 759-04-06.

The palace theater, which may be the oldest extant stage in the world using original backdrops and props, stands today exactly as it did on opening night in 1766. Here, 18th-century ballets and operas are still performed, authentic to the original costumes. Inquire at the Stockholm Information Service for a schedule of the period operas and ballets held from May to September. If no show is scheduled, the museum next door to the theater is definitely worth a peek.

Admission: 25 Kr ($4.55) for adults, 15 Kr ($2.70) for children.

Open: May–Aug, Mon–Sat 11:30am–4:30pm, Sun 12:30–4:30pm; Sept, daily 12:30–3pm. **Closed:** Oct–Apr.

CHINESE PAVILION (Kina Slott), in the palace park. Tel. 759-03-10.

Many of Europe's grand old palaces were inspired by the exotic architecture of Asia. This pavilion was constructed in Stockholm in 1753 as a royal birthday gift for the queen; it was quietly floated downriver so that it would surprise her when it arrived. The pavilion was a particular favorite of King Gustavus III, who loved to pass summer days here with his court.

Admission: 25 Kr ($4.55) for adults, 20 Kr ($3.65) for children.

Open: Apr, daily 1–3:30pm; May–Aug, daily 11am–4:30pm; Sept, Mon–Fri 1–3:30pm, Sat–Sun noon–3:30pm. **Closed:** Oct–Apr.

2. MARIEFRED

The perfect day trip, a visit to Mariefred on Lake Mälaren, includes a boat ride, a pretty little town that's easy to explore on foot, an old-timey train station and steam railway, a bookshop that's been around since 1897, and a castle with compelling nooks and crannies and a portrait collection from the 16th century to modern times.

GETTING THERE

In summer, a coal-fired steamboat called the S/S **Mariefred** makes the trip here from Stockholm; off-season, the sleek tour boat M/S **Kungsholm,** with two enclosed seating levels and a small open

IMPRESSIONS

The manners of Stockholm are refined, I hear, by the introduction of gallantry; but, in the country, romping and coarse freedoms, with coarse allusions, keep the spirits awake.
—MARY WOLLSTONECRAFT
(LETTERS WRITTEN DURING A SHORT RESIDENCE IN SWEDEN, ETC.,
1796)

---

deck, makes the journey. Both leave from the dock just east of City Hall. (Sit on the right-hand side for best views and photo opportunities.)

The pretty trip, which offers splendid views of City Hall as the boat leaves Stockholm, takes a little more than an hour and costs 80 Kr ($14.55), half price for children under 12. Snacks and drinks are served on board. (You may reboard the boat 10 minutes before departure time.) In summer you may also travel to Mariefred by train—the last leg of the trip, from Läggesta to Mariefred (change trains at the small terminal called Läggesta Södra), in a turn-of-the-century steam-powered train.

WHAT TO SEE & DO

Gripsholm Castle, located south of the town, is home to the **National Portrait Gallery,** with 1,200 of its 4,000 pictures on display. There are a number of rooms to see, outstanding among them Duke Karl's Chamber with its ceiling and paneling; Princess Sofia Albertina's Study with its tiled fireplace; the King's Bedchamber with its 17th-century ivory clock; the Council Chamber with its paneling and wall-hangings; the White Drawing Room; Gustav III's Theater with its domed ceiling; the Sentry Corridor (a portrait of Jenny Lind hangs here); the Large Gallery (portraits of King Carl XVI Gustaf and his family are here, along with one of Louisa Ulrika, whose attendants are depicted as hens); and the Tower Room, where you'll find modern portraits, including Dag Hammarskjöld, Greta Garbo, and Ingmar Bergman. Room 52 houses some compelling self-portraits.

A guidebook in English is helpful but pricey, at 25 Kr ($4.70). Admission is 20 Kr ($3.65) for adults, 5 Kr (90¢) for children under 16.

In the town of Mariefred, there are shops, an inviting café called **Konditori Fredman,** and the town hall, all around the main square, and some charming streets to explore behind it. The **Strand Restaurant,** in the yellow house by the water, serves more substantial meals.

Many visitors never realize the town has a **boardwalk** just beyond the restaurant (walk in the opposite direction of the church and the pier). The boardwalk leads past moored boats and houses with red-tile roofs peaking out to sea. There are benches where you can sit and gaze at the bullrushes and, beyond them, the church steeple and castle domes.

WHERE TO STAY

If you fall in love with Mariefred and yearn to stay an extra day or two, you can splurge and stay in **Gripsholms Värdshus,** Kyrkogatan 1 (Box 114, S-647 00, Mariefred; tel. 159-130-20; fax 159-109-74), a short walk from the ferry dock. Sweden's oldest inn, it has hosted kings and queens for nearly 400 years. After an extensive renovation, it reopened in 1989. The 30 double rooms and 15 suites, as well as the public rooms, have been decorated with furniture from different eras in the hotel's past. The dining room has a verandah that overlooks Gripsholm Bay. The hotel also has a less formal restaurant that is reminiscent of a country pub.

3. VAXHOLM

A popular island destination in the archipelago, this is a small place where you'll feel at home as soon as you arrive.

GETTING THERE

Local ferries and tour boats make the pleasant trip many times a day to Vaxholm. The ferry (tel. 14-09-60) leaves from in front of the Grand Hotel; the trip takes about an hour, calling at several islands along the way. Bus no. 670 will get you back to Stockholm if you don't want to wait for the return boat.

WHAT TO SEE & DO

To familiarize yourself with Vaxholm once you've disembarked, follow the path along the water, passing the sign for the fortress museum (see below), to the **lookout** at the old Portuguese battery. From this serene spot, you may stroll down the hill and sit on the rocks by the water.

From here, make your way to the **main square** of the town; follow Vallgatan, crossing Fiskaregatan and Kilgatan. Turn right on Lotsgatan, which leads to the main square and the **town hall,** built in 1885 and rebuilt in 1925. You'll also find some shops on the square. From here, follow Rådhusgatan back to the waterfront and the **information office.**

If you want to treat yourself to a good (but not inexpensive), elegantly served meal with a view of the harbor and boats scudding to and fro, visit the restaurant in the **Vaxholm Hotel.**

The **Vaxholm Fortress,** constructed between 1548 and 1863 to protect the inlet to Stockholm, is open from mid-May through August; admission is 10 Kr ($1.80) for adults, 5 Kr (90¢) for seniors and kids 7 to 12. The boat to the museum costs another 15 Kr ($2.70).

4. ARCHIPELAGO EXPLORATION

Vaxholm is only one of Greater Stockholm's 24,000 or so nearby islands. If you want to explore the archipelago in depth, buy a 16-day ferry pass, called **Båtluffarkortet,** for only 200 Kr ($36.40). Also drop by **Strömma Kanalbolaget,** Sweden's largest operator of archipelago tours, at Skeppsbron 30 (tel. 23-33-75), for a list of ferryboat cruises and timetables.

APPENDIX

A. BASIC PHRASES & VOCABULARY

ENGLISH	SWEDISH	PRONUNCIATION
Hello	**God dag**	goo *dah*
How are you?	**Hur står det till**	*hoor* store det till
Very well	**Tack bra**	tahk brah
Thank you	**Tack**	tahk
Goodbye	**Adjö**	ah-*yer*
Please	**Var snäll och**	vahr snell oh
Yes	**Ja**	yah
No	**Nej**	nay
Excuse me	**Ursäkta**	*oor*-sek-tah
I don't understand	**Jag förstår inte**	yah furst-*tore* in-tuh
Give me	**Ge mig**	yah may
Where is . . . ?	**Var finns det . . .?**	vahr finss det
the station	**stationen**	stah-shoo-nen
a hotel	**ett hotell**	et ho-*tel*
a restaurant	**en restaurang**	en rest-oh-*rahng*
a toilet	**toaletten**	twah-*let*-ten
To the right	**Åt höger**	oht *her*-ger
To the left	**Åt vänster**	oht *yen*-ster
Straight ahead	**Rakt fram**	rahkt-frahm
I would like . . .	**Jag vill ha . . .**	ya vill hah
to eat	**mat**	maht
a room	**ett rum**	et ruhm
How much is it?	**Vad kostar det?**	vahd *kaw*-stahr dayt
That's too expensive	**Det är för mycket**	dayt ayr fer *mik*-ket
When?	**Nä?**	nayr
Yesterday	**I går**	ee gore
Today	**I dag**	ee dah
Tomorrow	**I morgon**	ee *mawr*-rawn

NUMBERS

1 **ett (et)**	3 **tre (tray)**	5 **fem (fem)**
2 **tva (tvoh)**	4 **fyra (*fee*-rah)**	6 **sex (sex)**

7 **sju** (shew)	16 **sexton**	40 **fyrtio** (*fur*-tee)
8 **åtta** (awt-tah)	(*sex*-tawn)	50 **femtio**
9 **nio** (nee-joh)	17 **sjutton**	(*fem*-tee)
10 **tio** (*tee*-yoo)	(*shuht*-tawn)	60 **sextio**
11 **elva** (*el*-vah)	18 **aderton**	(*sex*-tee)
12 **tolv** (tawlv)	(*ahr*-tawn)	70 **sjuttio**
13 **tretton**	19 **nitton**	(*shut*-tee)
(*tret*-tawn)	(*nit*-tawn)	80 **åttio** (*awt*-tee)
14 **fjorton**	20 **tjugo**	90 **nittio**
(*fyoor*-tawn)	(*chew*-goo)	(*neet*-tee)
15 **femton**	30 **trettio**	100 **hundra**
(*fem*-tawn)	(*tret*-tee)	(huhn-dran)

B. MENU SAVVY

SOUPS

ärtsoppa pea soup
buljong broth

kålsoppa cabbage soup
soppa soup

FISH

anjovis anchovies
fisk fish
hummer lobster
kolja haddock
karp carp
kaviar caviar

makrill mackerel
ostron oyster
sill herring
stör sturgeon
torsk cod

MEATS

anka duck
biffstek steak
lammstek roast lamb
fläsk pork
gås goose
kalv veal
korv sausage

kyckling chicken
lamm lamb
lever liver
oxe beef
pytt i panna hash
rostbiff roast beef
skinka ham

VEGETABLES

ärttor peas
ärwskocka artichoke
blomkål cauliflower
brysselkål Brussels sprouts
grönsallad salad
gurka cucumber

kål cabbage
lök onion
morötter carrots
potatis potatoes
rödbetor beets
sparris asparagus

FRUITS

apelsiner oranges
avocado avocado
körsbär cherry
päron pear

persika peach
plommon plum
russin raisins
vindruva grape

DESSERTS

kakor pastry
russinkaka plumcake

sockerkaka cake

BEVERAGES

iste iced tea
juice juice
kaffe coffee
mineral vatten mineral water

mjölk milk
öl ale
te tea
vatten water

BASICS

bröd bread
knäckebröd crispbread
ost cheese
peppar pepper
pepparrot horseradish

salt salt
senap mustard
smör butter
socker sugar
vitlök garlic

C. METRIC MEASURES

LENGTH

1 millimeter	=	0.04 inches (or less than $\frac{1}{16}$ in)
1 centimeter	=	0.39 inches (or just under ½ in)
1 meter	=	1.09 yards (or about 39 inches)
1 kilometer	=	0.62 mile (or about ⅔ mile)

To convert kilometers to miles, take the number of kilometers and multiply by .62 (for example, 25km × .62 = 15.5 mi).

To convert miles to kilometers, take the number of miles and multiply by 1.61 (for example, 50 mi × 1.61 = 80.5km).

CAPACITY

1 liter = 33.92 ounces or 1.06 quarts or 0.26 gallons

To convert liters to gallons, take the number of liters and multiply by .26 (for example, 50 liters × .26 = 13 gallons).

To convert gallons to liters, take the number of gallons and multiply by 3.79 (for example, 10 gal × 3.79 = 37.9 liters).

WEIGHT

1 Gram	=	0.04 ounces (or about a paperclip's weight)
1 kilogram	=	2.2 pounds

To convert kilograms to pounds, take the number of kilos and multiply by 2.2 (for example, 75kg × 2.2 = 165 pounds).

To convert pounds to kilograms, take the number of pounds and multiply by .45 (for example, 90 pounds × .45 = 40.5kg).

TEMPERATURE

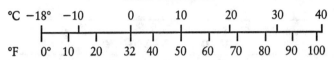

To convert degrees C to degrees F, multiply degrees C by 9, divide by 5, then add 32 (for example 20°C × 9/5 + 32 = 68°F).

To convert degrees F to degrees C, subtract 32 from degrees F, then multiply by 5, and divide by 9 (for example, 85°F − 32 × 5/9 = 29°C).

D. SIZE CONVERSIONS

The following charts should help you to choose the correct clothing sizes in Sweden. However, sizes can vary, so the best guide is simply to try things on.

WOMEN'S DRESSES, COATS & SKIRTS

American	3	5	7	9	11	12	13	14	15	16	18
Continental	36	38	38	40	40	42	42	44	44	46	48

WOMEN'S BLOUSES & SWEATERS

American	6	8	10	12	14	16
Continental	34	36	38	40	42	44

WOMEN'S SHOES

American	5	6	7	8	9	10
Continental	36	37	38	39	40	41

MEN'S SUITS

American	34	36	38	40	42	44	46	48
Continental	44	46	48	50	52	54	56	58

MEN'S SHIRTS

American	14½	15	15½	16	16½	17	17½	18
Continental	37	38	39	41	42	43	44	45

MENS' SHOES

American	7	8	9	10	11	12	13
Continental	39½	41	42	43	44½	46	47

MEN'S HATS

American	6⅞	7⅛	7¼	7⅜	7½	7⅝
Continental	55	56	58	59	60	61

CHILDREN'S CLOTHING

American	3	4	5	6	6X
Continental	98	104	110	116	122

CHILDREN'S SHOES

American	8	9	10	11	12	13	1	2	3
Continental	24	25	27	28	29	30	32	33	34

INDEX

GENERAL INFORMATION

SIGHTS & ATTRACTIONS

STOCKHOLM

EXCURSION AREAS

ACCOMMODATIONS

STOCKHOLM

MARIEFRED

RESTAURANTS

NOW, SAVE MONEY ON ALL YOUR TRAVELS!
Join Frommer's™ Dollarwise® Travel Club

Saving money while traveling is never easy, which is why the **Dollarwise Travel Club** was formed 32 years ago to provide cost-cutting travel strategies, up-to-date travel information, and a sense of community for value-conscious travelers from all over the world.

In keeping with the money-saving concept, the annual membership fee is low—$20 for U.S. residents and $25 for residents of Canada, Mexico, and other countries—and is immediately exceeded by the value of your benefits, which include:

1. Any TWO books listed on the following pages;
2. Plus any ONE Frommer's City Guide;
3. A subscription to our quarterly newspaper, *The Dollarwise Traveler;*
4. A membership card that entitles you to purchase through the Club all Frommer's publications for 33% to 40% off their retail price.

The eight-page *Dollarwise Traveler* tells you about the latest developments in good-value travel worldwide and includes the following columns: **Hospitality Exchange** (for those offering and seeking hospitality in cities all over the world); and **Share-a-Trip** (for those looking for travel companions to share costs).

Aside from the various Frommer's Guides, the Gault Millau Guides, and the Real Guides you can also choose from our Special Editions, which include such titles as *Caribbean Hideaways* (the 100 most romantic places to stay in the Islands); and *Marilyn Wood's Wonderful Weekends* (a selection of the best mini-vacations within a 200-mile radius of New York City).

To join this Club, send the appropriate membership fee with your name and address to: Frommer's Dollarwise Travel Club, 15 Columbus Circle, New York, NY 10023. Remember to specify which single city guide and which two other guides you wish to receive in your initial package of member's benefits. Or tear out the pages, check off your choices, and send them to us with your membership fee.

FROMMER BOOKS
PRENTICE HALL TRAVEL   Date_____
15 COLUMBUS CIRCLE
NEW YORK, NY 10023

Friends: Please send me the books checked below.

FROMMER'S™ COMPREHENSIVE GUIDES
(Guides listing facilities from budget to deluxe, with emphasis on the medium-priced)

☐ Alaska	$14.95	☐ Italy	$19.00
☐ Australia	$14.95	☐ Japan & Hong Kong	$17.00
☐ Austria & Hungary	$14.95	☐ Morocco	$18.00
☐ Belgium, Holland & Luxembourg	$14.95	☐ Nepal	$18.00
☐ Bermuda & The Bahamas	$17.00	☐ New England	$17.00
☐ Brazil	$14.95	☐ New Mexico	$13.95
☐ California	$18.00	☐ New York State	$19.00
☐ Canada	$16.00	☐ Northwest	$16.95
☐ Caribbean	$17.00	☐ Puerta Vallarta (avail. Feb. '92)	$14.00
☐ Carolinas & Georgia	$17.00	☐ Portugal, Madeira & the Azores	$14.95
☐ Colorado (avail. Jan '92)	$14.00	☐ Scandinavia	$18.95
☐ Cruises (incl. Alaska, Carib, Mex, Hawaii, Panama, Canada & US)	$16.00	☐ Scotland (avail. Feb. '92)	$17.00
		☐ South Pacific	$20.00
☐ Delaware, Maryland, Pennsylvania & the New Jersey Shore (avail. Jan. '92)	$19.00	☐ Southeast Asia	$14.95
		☐ Switzerland & Liechtenstein	$19.00
☐ Egypt	$14.95	☐ Thailand	$20.00
☐ England	$17.00	☐ Virginia (avail. Feb. '92)	$14.00
☐ Florida	$17.00	☐ Virgin Islands	$13.00
☐ France	$15.95	☐ USA	$16.95
☐ Germany	$18.00		

0891492

☐ Paris Rendez-Vous $10.95	☐ Travel Diary and Record Book. $5.95
☐ Swap and Go (Home Exchanging). $10.95	☐ Where to Stay USA (from $3 to $30 a
	night). $13.95

FROMMER'S TOURING GUIDES

(Color illustrated guides that include walking tours, cultural and historic sites, and practical information)

☐ Amsterdam. $10.95	☐ New York $10.95
☐ Australia $12.95	☐ Paris $8.95
☐ Brazil. $10.95	☐ Rome. $10.95
☐ Egypt. $8.95	☐ Scotland. $9.95
☐ Florence. $8.95	☐ Thailand. $12.95
☐ Hong Kong $10.95	☐ Turkey $10.95
☐ London $12.95	☐ Venice $8.95

GAULT MILLAU

(The only guides that distinguish the truly superlative from the merely overrated)

☐ The Best of Chicago $15.95	☐ The Best of Los Angeles $16.95
☐ The Best of Florida $17.00	☐ The Best of New England $15.95
☐ The Best of France $16.95	☐ The Best of New Orleans. $16.95
☐ The Best of Germany $18.00	☐ The Best of New York $16.95
☐ The Best of Hawaii $16.95	☐ The Best of Paris $16.95
☐ The Best of Hong Kong $16.95	☐ The Best of San Francisco $16.95
☐ The Best of Italy. $16.95	☐ The Best of Thailand. $17.95
☐ The Best of London $16.95	☐ The Best of Toronto $17.00
	☐ The Best of Washington, D.C. $16.95

THE REAL GUIDES

(Opinionated, politically aware guides for youthful budget-minded travelers)

☐ Amsterdam $9.95	☐ Mexico. $11.95
☐ Berlin. $11.95	☐ Morocco $12.95
☐ Brazil. $13.95	☐ New York $9.95
☐ California & the West Coast $11.95	☐ Paris $9.95
☐ Czechoslovakia $13.95	☐ Peru. $12.95
☐ France $12.95	☐ Poland $13.95
☐ Germany $13.95	☐ Portugal. $10.95
☐ Greece. $13.95	☐ San Francisco $11.95
☐ Guatemala $13.95	☐ Scandinavia $14.95
☐ Hong Kong $11.95	☐ Spain $12.95
☐ Hungary $12.95	☐ Turkey $12.95
☐ Ireland. $12.95	☐ Venice $11.95
☐ Italy. $13.95	☐ Women Travel $12.95
☐ Kenya. $12.95	☐ Yugoslavia $12.95

ORDER NOW!

In U.S. include $2 shipping UPS for 1st book; $1 ea. add'l book. Outside U.S. $3 and $1, respectively.

Allow four to six weeks for delivery in U.S., longer outside U.S. We discourage rush order service, but orders arriving with shipping fees plus a $15 surcharge will be handled as rush orders.

Enclosed is my check or money order for $_____

NAME _____

ADDRESS _____

CITY _____ STATE _____ ZIP _____

0891492